CLASSIC
RECIPES™

Publications International, Ltd.

Favorite Brand Name Recipes at www.fbnr.com

Microwave Cooking: Microwave ovens vary in wattage. Use the cooking times as guidelines and check for doneness before adding more time.

Preparation/Cooking Times: Preparation times are based on the approximate amount of time required to assemble the recipe before cooking, baking, chilling or serving. These times include preparation steps such as measuring, chopping and mixing. The fact that some preparations and cooking can be done simultaneously is taken into account. Preparation of optional ingredients and serving suggestions is not included.

Contents

AMAZING
DIPS & APPETIZERS

A great party starts with great food, including everybody's favorite, Lipton® Onion Dip. But there's more to Lipton® Recipe Secrets® Soup Mix than just dips. Any of the savory appetizers, creamy spreads and tasty snacks found in this chapter will elevate your gathering to a special occasion.

7-Layer Ranch Dip

1 envelope LIPTON® RECIPE SECRETS® Ranch Soup Mix
1 container (16 ounces) sour cream
1 cup shredded lettuce
1 medium tomato, chopped (about 1 cup)
1 can (2.25 ounces) sliced pitted ripe olives, drained
¼ cup chopped red onion
1 can (4.5 ounces) chopped green chilies, drained
1 cup shredded Cheddar cheese (about 4 ounces)

1. In 2-quart shallow dish, combine soup mix and sour cream.

2. Evenly layer remaining ingredients, ending with cheese. Chill, if desired. Serve with tortilla chips.   *Makes 7 cups dip*

7-Layer Ranch Dip

Helpful Hint:
Serve this delicious pizza as a main dish by cutting it into Sicilian-style square pieces.

Sweet Pepper Pizza Fingers

2 tablespoons margarine or butter
2 large red, green and/or yellow bell peppers, thinly sliced
1 clove garlic, finely chopped
1 envelope LIPTON® RECIPE SECRETS® Onion Soup Mix
1 cup water
1 package (10 ounces) refrigerated pizza crust dough
1½ cups shredded mozzarella cheese (about 6 ounces), divided

1. Preheat oven to 425°F.

2. In 12-inch skillet, melt margarine over medium heat; cook peppers and garlic, stirring occasionally, 5 minutes or until peppers are tender. Stir in soup mix blended with water. Bring to a boil over high heat. Reduce heat to low and simmer uncovered, 6 minutes or until liquid is absorbed. Remove from heat; set aside to cool 5 minutes.

3. Meanwhile, on baking sheet sprayed with nonstick cooking spray, roll out pizza dough into 12×8-inch rectangle. Sprinkle 1 cup mozzarella cheese over dough; top with cooked pepper mixture, spreading to edges of dough. Top with remaining ½ cup mozzarella cheese. Bake 10 minutes or until crust is golden brown and topping is bubbly. Remove from oven and let stand 5 minutes. To serve, cut into 4×1-inch strips.

Makes about 24 appetizers

PREP TIME: 5 MINUTES

Salsa Onion Dip

1 envelope LIPTON® RECIPE SECRETS® Onion Soup Mix
1 container (16 ounces) sour cream
½ cup salsa

1. In medium bowl, combine all ingredients; chill, if desired.

2. Serve with your favorite dippers.

Makes 2½ cups dip

Can't Get Enough Chicken Wings

  18 chicken wings (about 3 pounds)
   1 envelope LIPTON® RECIPE SECRETS® Savory Herb with Garlic
      Soup Mix
  ½ cup water
   2 to 3 tablespoons hot pepper sauce* (optional)
   2 tablespoons margarine or butter

Use more or less hot pepper sauce as desired.

1. Cut tips off chicken wings (save tips for soup). Cut chicken wings in half at joint. Deep fry, bake or broil until golden brown and crunchy.

2. Meanwhile, in small saucepan, combine soup mix, water and hot pepper sauce. Cook over low heat, stirring occasionally, 2 minutes or until thickened. Remove from heat and stir in margarine.

3. In large bowl, toss cooked chicken wings with hot soup mixture until evenly coated. Serve, if desired, over greens with cut-up celery.

Makes 36 appetizers

Lipton® Ranch Dip

1 envelope LIPTON® RECIPE SECRETS® Ranch Soup Mix
1 container (16 ounces) sour cream

1. In medium bowl, combine ingredients; chill, if desired.

2. Serve with your favorite dippers.   *Makes 2 cups dip*

Ranch Salsa Dip: Stir in ½ cup of your favorite salsa.

Ranch Artichoke Dip: Stir in 1 jar (14 ounces) marinated artichoke hearts, drained and chopped.

Four Cheese Spread

1 package (8 ounces) cream cheese, softened
1 cup shredded Swiss cheese (about 4 ounces)
1 cup shredded fontina or Monterey Jack cheese (about 3 ounces)
½ cup sour cream
¼ cup grated Parmesan cheese
¼ cup finely chopped fresh basil leaves *or* 1½ teaspoons dried basil leaves, crushed
1 tablespoon finely chopped fresh parsley
1 tablespoon lemon juice
1 envelope LIPTON® RECIPE SECRETS® Vegetable Soup Mix

1. Line 4-cup mold or bowl with waxed paper or dampened cheese cloth; set aside.

2. With food processor or electric mixer, combine all ingredients until smooth. Pack into prepared mold; cover and chill. To serve, unmold onto serving platter and remove waxed paper. Garnish, if desired, with additional chopped parsley and basil. Serve, if desired, with assorted crackers, bagel chips or cucumber slices.   *Makes about 3½ cups spread*

Top to bottom: Lipton® Onion Dip (page 23) and Lipton® Ranch Dip

Party Stuffed Pinwheels

1 envelope LIPTON® RECIPE SECRETS® Savory Herb with Garlic Soup Mix*

1 package (8 ounces) cream cheese, softened

1 cup shredded mozzarella cheese (about 4 ounces)

2 tablespoons milk

1 tablespoon grated Parmesan cheese

2 packages (10 ounces each) refrigerated pizza crust dough

*Also terrific with LIPTON® RECIPE SECRETS® Onion Soup Mix.

1. Preheat oven to 425°F. In medium bowl, combine all ingredients except pizza dough; set aside.

2. Unroll pizza dough, then top evenly with filling. Roll, starting at longest side, jelly-roll style. Cut each roll into 16 rounds. (If rolled pizza dough is too soft to cut, refrigerate or freeze until firm.)

3. On baking sheet sprayed with nonstick cooking spray, arrange rounds cut side down.

4. Bake uncovered, 13 minutes or until golden brown.

Makes 32 pinwheels

Home-Style Corn Cakes

1 cup yellow cornmeal

½ cup all-purpose flour

½ teaspoon baking powder

½ teaspoon baking soda

1 envelope LIPTON® RECIPE SECRETS® Onion Soup Mix*

¾ cup buttermilk

1 egg, beaten

1 can (14¾ ounces) cream-style corn

2 ounces roasted red peppers, chopped (about ¼ cup)

   I CAN'T BELIEVE IT'S NOT BUTTER!® Spread

*Also terrific with LIPTON® RECIPE SECRETS® Golden Onion Soup Mix.

1. In large bowl, combine cornmeal, flour, baking powder and baking soda. Blend soup mix with buttermilk, egg, corn and roasted red peppers; stir into cornmeal mixture.

2. In 12-inch nonstick skillet or on griddle, melt ½ teaspoon I Can't Believe It's Not Butter!® Spread over medium heat. Drop ¼ cup batter for each corn cake and cook, turning once, 5 minutes or until cooked through and golden brown. Remove to serving platter and keep warm. Repeat with remaining batter and additional I Can't Believe It's Not Butter!® Spread if needed. Serve, if desired, with sour cream and salsa.

Makes about 18 corn cakes

Helpful Hint:
Leftover corn cakes can be wrapped and frozen. Remove them from the wrapping and reheat them straight from the freezer in a preheated 350°F oven for about 15 minutes.

Cool Wings with Hot Sauce

18 chicken wings (about 3 pounds)
1 envelope LIPTON® RECIPE SECRETS® Ranch Soup Mix
½ cup water
2 tablespoons margarine or butter
Red or green cayenne pepper sauce

1. Cut tips off chicken wings (save tips for soup). Cut chicken wings in half at joints. Deep fry, bake or broil until golden brown and crunchy.

2. Meanwhile, in small saucepan, combine soup mix and water. Cook over low heat, stirring occasionally, 2 minutes or until thickened. Remove from heat and stir in margarine until melted.

3. In large bowl, toss cooked chicken wings with hot soup mixture until evenly coated. Serve with cayenne pepper sauce and, if desired, cut-up celery.

Makes 36 appetizers

PREP TIME: 5 MINUTES
BAKE TIME: 20 MINUTES

Ranch Bacon Cheddar Dip

2 packages (8 ounces each) cream cheese, softened
¾ cup milk
1 envelope LIPTON® RECIPE SECRETS® Ranch Soup Mix
2 cups shredded Cheddar cheese (about 8 ounces)
2 tablespoons bacon bits or crumbled bacon

1. Preheat oven to 325°F. In medium bowl, with electric mixer, beat cream cheese until smooth and fluffy, about 2 minutes. Stir in milk, soup mix, cheese and bacon bits.

2. Transfer to a lightly greased shallow 1-quart casserole. Bake uncovered, 20 to 25 minutes or until heated through. Stir before serving.

3. Serve, if desired, with tortilla chips.

Makes about 3 cups dip

Savory Onion Crab Cakes over Greens

- 1 envelope LIPTON® RECIPE SECRETS® Onion Soup Mix
- 1 cup plain dry bread crumbs
- 1 can (6 ounces) refrigerated pasteurized crabmeat or 1 package (6 ounces) frozen crabmeat, thawed and drained
- 1 medium red, orange or yellow bell pepper, finely chopped
- 2 eggs
- 2 tablespoons HELLMANN'S® or BEST FOODS® Real Mayonnaise
- 2 teaspoons red or green cayenne pepper sauce
  All-purpose flour
- 4 teaspoons BERTOLLI® Olive Oil, divided
- 8 cups assorted baby greens
  Your favorite vinaigrette dressing

1. In medium bowl, combine soup mix, bread crumbs, crabmeat, bell pepper, eggs, mayonnaise and cayenne pepper sauce. Shape into 12 small patties. Lightly flour both sides.

2. In 12-inch nonstick skillet, heat 2 teaspoons olive oil over medium-high heat and cook 6 crab cakes 3½ minutes or until golden brown, turning once. Remove from skillet and keep warm. Repeat with remaining olive oil and patties.

3. To serve, on 4 plates, arrange baby greens. Arrange 3 crab cakes on each salad and drizzle with dressing.   *Makes 4 servings*

White Pizza Dip

1 envelope LIPTON® RECIPE SECRETS® Savory Herb with Garlic Soup Mix
1 container (16 ounces) sour cream
1 cup (8 ounces) ricotta cheese
1 cup shredded mozzarella cheese (about 4 ounces), divided
¼ cup (1 ounce) chopped pepperoni (optional)
1 loaf Italian or French bread, sliced

1. Preheat oven to 350°F. In shallow 1-quart casserole, combine soup mix, sour cream, ricotta cheese, ¾ cup mozzarella cheese and pepperoni.

2. Sprinkle with remaining ¼ cup mozzarella cheese.

3. Bake uncovered, 30 minutes or until heated through. Serve with bread.

Makes 3 cups dip

Chicken Quesadillas

2 tablespoons margarine or butter

1 pound boneless, skinless chicken breast halves, sliced

1 envelope LIPTON® RECIPE SECRETS® Onion Soup Mix

4 flour tortillas

1 package (8 ounces) shredded mozzarella or Monterey Jack cheese

1 medium tomato, chopped (optional)

1. Preheat broiler. In 12-inch nonstick skillet, over medium-high heat, melt margarine. Add chicken and soup mix. Cook 5 minutes, stirring occasionally, until chicken is thoroughly cooked.

2. On baking sheet, arrange 2 tortillas. Top each with ½ cup cheese, half of chicken mixture, chopped tomato and additional ½ cup cheese. Top with remaining tortillas.

3. Place tortillas under broiler 2 to 3 minutes or until cheese is melted and tortillas are lightly browned, turning once. Cut each tortilla into 8 wedges. Serve, if desired, with sour cream and chopped cilantro.

Makes 16 wedges

Vegetable Cream Cheese

PREP TIME: 10 MINUTES
CHILL TIME: 2 HOURS

1 envelope LIPTON® RECIPE SECRETS® Vegetable Soup Mix

2 packages (8 ounces each) cream cheese, softened

2 tablespoons milk

1. In medium bowl, combine all ingredients; chill 2 hours.

2. Serve on bagels or with assorted fresh vegetables.

Makes 2½ cups spread

Creamy Garlic Salsa Dip

1 envelope LIPTON® RECIPE SECRETS® Savory Herb with Garlic Soup Mix*

1 container (16 ounces) sour cream

½ cup your favorite salsa

Also terrific with LIPTON® RECIPE SECRETS® Onion Soup Mix.

1. In medium bowl, combine all ingredients; chill, if desired.

2. Serve with your favorite dippers.   *Makes 2½ cups dip*

Mini Cocktail Meatballs

1 envelope LIPTON® RECIPE SECRETS® Onion, Onion Mushroom or Beefy Onion Soup Mix

1 pound ground beef

½ cup plain dry bread crumbs

¼ cup dry red wine or water

2 eggs, lightly beaten

1. Preheat oven to 375°F.

2. In medium bowl, combine all ingredients; shape into 1-inch meatballs.

3. In shallow baking pan, arrange meatballs and bake 18 minutes or until done. Serve, if desired, with assorted mustards or tomato sauce.

Makes about 4 dozen meatballs

Savory Chicken Satay

1 envelope LIPTON® RECIPE SECRETS® Onion Soup Mix

¼ cup BERTOLLI® Olive Oil

2 tablespoons firmly packed brown sugar

2 tablespoons SKIPPY® Peanut Butter

1 pound boneless, skinless chicken breasts, pounded and cut into thin strips

12 to 16 large wooden skewers, soaked in water

1. In large plastic bag, combine soup mix, oil, brown sugar and peanut butter. Add chicken and toss to coat well. Close bag and marinate in refrigerator 30 minutes.

2. Remove chicken from marinade, discarding marinade. On skewers, thread chicken, weaving back and forth.

3. Grill or broil skewers until chicken is thoroughly cooked. Serve with your favorite dipping sauces.   *Makes 12 to 16 appetizers*

Zesty Bruschetta

1 envelope LIPTON® RECIPE SECRETS® Savory Herb with Garlic Soup Mix
6 tablespoons BERTOLLI® Olive Oil*
1 loaf French or Italian bread (about 18 inches long), sliced lengthwise
2 tablespoons shredded or grated Parmesan cheese

Substitution: Use ½ cup margarine or butter, melted.

1. Preheat oven to 350°F. Blend soup mix and oil. Brush onto bread, then sprinkle with cheese.

2. Bake 12 minutes or until golden. Slice, then serve.

Makes about 18 pieces

Polenta Triangles

3 cups cold water
1 cup yellow cornmeal
1 envelope LIPTON® RECIPE SECRETS® Golden Onion or Onion Soup Mix
1 can (4 ounces) mild chopped green chilies, drained
½ cup thawed frozen or drained canned whole kernel corn
⅓ cup finely chopped roasted red peppers
½ cup shredded sharp Cheddar cheese (about 2 ounces)

1. In 3-quart saucepan, bring water to a boil over high heat. With wire whisk, stir in cornmeal, then soup mix. Reduce heat to low and simmer uncovered, stirring constantly, 25 minutes or until thickened. Stir in chilies, corn and roasted red peppers.

2. Spread into lightly greased 9-inch square baking pan; sprinkle with cheese. Let stand 20 minutes or until firm; cut into triangles. Serve at room temperature or heat in oven at 350°F for 5 minutes or until warm.

Makes about 24 triangles

Buffalo Wings

  1 envelope LIPTON® RECIPE SECRETS® Golden Onion Soup Mix*
  ½ cup I CAN'T BELIEVE IT'S NOT BUTTER!® Spread, melted
  2 tablespoons white vinegar
  2 tablespoons water
  2 cloves garlic
  1½ to 2 teaspoons ground red pepper
  1 teaspoon ground cumin (optional)
  24 chicken wings (about 4 pounds)
  1 cup WISH-BONE® Chunky Blue Cheese Dressing
Also terrific with LIPTON® RECIPE SECRETS® Onion Soup Mix.

1. In food processor or blender, process soup mix, I Can't Believe It's Not Butter!® Spread, vinegar, water, garlic, pepper and cumin until blended; set aside.

2. Cut tips off chicken wings (save tips for soup). Cut chicken wings in half at joints. Broil chicken 12 minutes or until brown, turning after 6 minutes. Brush with half of the soup mixture, then broil 2 minutes or until crisp. Turn, then brush with remaining soup mixture and broil 1 minute. Serve with Wish-Bone® Chunky Blue Cheese Dressing and, if desired, celery sticks.

Makes 48 appetizers

Lipton® Onion Dip

PREP TIME: 5 MINUTES

  1 envelope LIPTON® RECIPE SECRETS® Onion Soup Mix
  1 container (16 ounces) sour cream

1. In medium bowl, combine ingredients; chill, if desired.

2. Serve with your favorite dippers.

Makes 2 cups dip

Hot Artichoke Dip

Helpful Hint:

When serving hot dip for a party, try baking it in two smaller casseroles. When the first casserole is empty, replace it with the second one, fresh from the oven.

1 envelope LIPTON® RECIPE SECRETS® Onion Soup Mix*
1 can (14 ounces) artichoke hearts, drained and chopped
1 cup HELLMANN'S® or BEST FOODS® Real Mayonnaise
1 container (8 ounces) sour cream
1 cup shredded Swiss or mozzarella cheese (about 4 ounces)

Also terrific with LIPTON® RECIPE SECRETS® Savory Herb with Garlic, Golden Onion or Onion Mushroom Soup Mix.

1. Preheat oven to 350°F. In 1-quart casserole, combine all ingredients.

2. Bake uncovered, 30 minutes or until heated through.

3. Serve with your favorite dippers. *Makes 3 cups dip*

Cold Artichoke Dip: Omit Swiss cheese. Stir in, if desired, ¼ cup grated Parmesan cheese. Do not bake.

Pecan Cheese Ball

2 packages (8 ounces each) cream cheese, softened
1 package (8 ounces) shredded Cheddar cheese
1 envelope LIPTON® RECIPE SECRETS® Onion Soup Mix
2 tablespoons finely chopped fresh parsley
½ teaspoon garlic powder
½ cup finely chopped pecans, toasted, if desired

1. In large bowl, with electric mixer, beat cream cheese until light and fluffy, about 2 minutes. Stir in Cheddar cheese, soup mix, parsley and garlic powder.

2. Wet hands with cold water. Shape cheese mixture into ball. Roll cheese ball in pecans until evenly coated.

3. Refrigerate 1 hour or until set. Serve with crackers.

Makes 1 cheese ball

Caponata Spread

1½ tablespoons BERTOLLI® Olive Oil
1 medium eggplant, diced (about 4 cups)
1 medium onion, chopped
1½ cups water, divided
1 envelope LIPTON® RECIPE SECRETS® Savory Herb with Garlic Soup Mix
2 tablespoons chopped fresh parsley (optional)
Salt and ground black pepper to taste
Pita chips or thinly sliced Italian or French bread

1. In 10-inch nonstick skillet, heat oil over medium heat and cook eggplant with onion 3 minutes. Add ½ cup water. Reduce heat to low and simmer covered, 3 minutes.

2. Stir in soup mix blended with remaining 1 cup water. Bring to a boil over high heat. Reduce heat to low and simmer uncovered, stirring occasionally, 20 minutes.

3. Stir in parsley, salt and pepper. Serve with pita chips.

Makes about 4 cups spread

Roasted Red Pepper Dip

1 envelope LIPTON® RECIPE SECRETS® Onion Soup Mix
1 container (16 ounces) sour cream
1 jar (7 ounces) roasted red peppers, drained and chopped

1. In large bowl, combine all ingredients; chill, if desired.

2. Serve, if desired, with bread sticks, celery or carrot sticks, cooked tortellini or mozzarella sticks.

Makes 2 cups dip

Hearty Nachos

PREP TIME: 10 MINUTES
COOK TIME: 12 MINUTES

1 pound ground beef

1 envelope LIPTON® RECIPE SECRETS® Onion Soup Mix

1 can (19 ounces) black beans, rinsed and drained

1 cup salsa

1 package (8½ ounces) plain tortilla chips

1 cup shredded Cheddar cheese (about 4 ounces)

1. In 12-inch nonstick skillet, brown ground beef over medium-high heat; drain.

2. Stir in soup mix, black beans and salsa. Bring to a boil over high heat. Reduce heat to low and simmer 5 minutes or until heated through.

3. Arrange tortilla chips on serving platter. Spread beef mixture over chips; sprinkle with Cheddar cheese. Top, if desired, with sliced green onions, sliced pitted ripe olives, chopped tomato and chopped cilantro.

Makes 8 servings

Helpful Hint:

To crush the tortilla chips quickly and easily, place them in a sealed food storage bag and then run a rolling pin over the bag several times to pulverize them.

Tortilla Crunch Chicken Fingers

1 envelope LIPTON® RECIPE SECRETS® Savory Herb with Garlic Soup Mix
1 cup finely crushed plain tortilla chips or cornflakes (about 3 ounces)
1½ pounds boneless, skinless chicken breasts, cut into strips
1 egg
2 tablespoons water
2 tablespoons I CAN'T BELIEVE IT'S NOT BUTTER!® Spread, melted

1. Preheat oven to 400°F.

2. In medium bowl, combine soup mix and tortilla chips. In large plastic bag or bowl, combine chicken and egg beaten with water until evenly coated. Remove chicken and dip in tortilla mixture until evenly coated; discard bag. On 15½×10½×1-inch jelly-roll pan sprayed with nonstick cooking spray, arrange chicken; drizzle with I Can't Believe It's Not Butter!® Spread. Bake uncovered, 12 minutes or until chicken is thoroughly cooked. Serve, if desired, with chunky salsa.   *Makes about 24 chicken fingers*

PREP TIME: 10 MINUTES

BLT Dip

1 envelope LIPTON® RECIPE SECRETS® Onion Soup Mix*
1 container (8 ounces) sour cream
1 cup HELLMANN'S® or BEST FOODS® Real Mayonnaise
1 medium tomato, chopped (about 1 cup)
½ cup cooked crumbled bacon (about 6 slices) or bacon bits
   Shredded lettuce

Also terrific with LIPTON® RECIPE SECRETS® Golden Onion Soup Mix.

1. In medium bowl, combine all ingredients except lettuce; chill, if desired.

2. Garnish with lettuce and serve with your favorite dippers.

Makes 3 cups dip

SAVORY
VEGETABLES
& SIDES

Dinnertime just wouldn't be complete without a delicious side dish or two. Mashed potatoes, herb stuffing, roasted vegetables and rice pilaf are just a few possibilities. With these easy-to-prepare dishes, the hardest part will be choosing which recipe to make!

Savory Skillet Broccoli

PREP TIME: 5 MINUTES
COOK TIME: 10 MINUTES

    1 tablespoon BERTOLLI® Olive Oil
    6 cups fresh broccoli florets *or* 1 pound green beans, trimmed
    1 envelope LIPTON® RECIPE SECRETS® Golden Onion Soup Mix*
  1½ cups water

Also terrific with LIPTON® RECIPE SECRETS® Onion Mushroom Soup Mix.

1. In 12-inch skillet, heat oil over medium-high heat and cook broccoli, stirring occasionally, 2 minutes.

2. Stir in soup mix blended with water. Bring to a boil over high heat.

3. Reduce heat to medium-low and simmer covered, 6 minutes or until broccoli is tender.
                           Makes 4 servings

Savory Skillet Broccoli

Quick Corn Bread with Chilies 'n' Cheese

1 package (12 to 16 ounces) corn bread or corn muffin mix, plus
    ingredients to prepare mix
1 cup (4 ounces) shredded Monterey Jack cheese, divided
1 can (4 ounces) chopped green chilies, drained
1 envelope LIPTON® RECIPE SECRETS® Vegetable Soup Mix

1. Prepare corn bread mix according to package directions; stir in ½ cup cheese, chilies and soup mix.

2. Spread batter in lightly greased 8-inch square baking pan; bake as directed. While warm, top with remaining ½ cup cheese. Cool completely on wire rack. To serve, cut into squares.   *Makes 16 servings*

Lipton® California Mashed Potatoes

2 pounds all-purpose potatoes, peeled, if desired, and cut into
    chunks
    Water
2 tablespoons chopped fresh parsley (optional)
1 envelope LIPTON® RECIPE SECRETS® Onion Soup Mix*
¾ cup milk, warmed
½ cup sour cream

Also terrific with LIPTON® RECIPE SECRETS® Golden Onion or Savory Herb with Garlic Soup Mix.

1. In 3-quart saucepan, cover potatoes with water. Bring to a boil over high heat. Reduce heat to low and simmer 20 minutes or until potatoes are very tender; drain.

2. Return potatoes to saucepan. Mash potatoes. Stir in parsley, soup mix blended with milk and sour cream.   *Makes about 6 servings*

Quick Corn Bread with Chilies 'n' Cheese

Oven-Roasted Vegetables

    1 envelope LIPTON® RECIPE SECRETS® Savory Herb with Garlic
        Soup Mix*
1½ pounds assorted fresh vegetables**
    2 tablespoons BERTOLLI® Olive Oil

Also terrific with LIPTON® RECIPE SECRETS® Onion or Golden Onion Soup Mix.
**Use any combination of the following, sliced: zucchini; yellow squash; red, green or yellow bell peppers; carrots; celery or mushrooms.*

1. Preheat oven to 450°F. In large plastic bag or bowl, combine all ingredients. Close bag and shake, or toss in bowl, until vegetables are evenly coated.

2. In 13×9-inch baking or roasting pan, arrange vegetables; discard bag.

3. Bake uncovered, stirring once, 20 minutes or until vegetables are tender.

Makes 4 servings

PREP TIME: 5 MINUTES
COOK TIME: 25 MINUTES

Simple Savory Rice

2½ cups water
    1 envelope LIPTON® RECIPE SECRETS® Soup Mix (any variety)
    1 cup uncooked regular or converted rice

1. In 2-quart saucepan, bring water to a boil over high heat. Stir in soup mix and rice.

2. Reduce heat and simmer covered, 20 minutes or until rice is tender.

Makes 3 servings

Oven-Roasted Vegetables

Garlic Mashed Potatoes

6 medium all-purpose potatoes, peeled, if desired, and cut into
     chunks (about 3 pounds)
  Water
1 envelope LIPTON® RECIPE SECRETS® Savory Herb with Garlic
     Soup Mix*
½ cup milk
½ cup I CAN'T BELIEVE IT'S NOT BUTTER!® Spread

Also terrific with LIPTON® RECIPE SECRETS® Onion or Golden Onion Soup Mix.

1. In 4-quart saucepan, cover potatoes with water; bring to a boil.

2. Reduce heat to low and simmer uncovered, 20 minutes or until potatoes
are very tender; drain.

3. Return potatoes to saucepan, then mash. Stir in remaining ingredients.

Makes 8 servings

Broccoli Casserole with Crumb Topping

2 slices day-old white bread, coarsely crumbled (about 1¼ cups)

½ cup shredded mozzarella cheese (about 2 ounces)

2 tablespoons chopped fresh parsley (optional)

2 tablespoons BERTOLLI® Olive Oil, divided

1 clove garlic, finely chopped

6 cups broccoli florets and/or cauliflowerets

1 envelope LIPTON® RECIPE SECRETS® Onion Soup Mix

1 cup water

1 large tomato, chopped

1. In small bowl, combine bread crumbs, cheese, parsley, 1 tablespoon oil and garlic; set aside.

2. In 12-inch skillet, heat remaining 1 tablespoon oil over medium heat and cook broccoli, stirring frequently, 2 minutes.

3. Stir in soup mix blended with water. Bring to a boil over high heat. Reduce heat to low and simmer uncovered, stirring occasionally, 8 minutes or until broccoli is almost tender. Add tomato and simmer 2 minutes.

4. Spoon vegetable mixture into 1½-quart casserole; top with bread crumb mixture. Broil 1½ minutes or until crumbs are golden and cheese is melted.

Makes 6 servings

Fresh Vegetables over Couscous

3 tablespoons BERTOLLI® Olive Oil

2 pounds assorted fresh vegetables*

1 can (15 to 19 ounces) chickpeas or garbanzos, rinsed and drained

¼ cup golden raisins (optional)

1 envelope LIPTON® RECIPE SECRETS® Savory Herb with Garlic Soup Mix

1½ cups water

1 to 2 tablespoons lemon juice

½ teaspoon ground cumin (optional)

1 box (10 ounces) couscous, prepared according to package directions

Use any combination of the following, sliced: zucchini; yellow squash; red onions; red or green bell peppers; carrots or mushrooms.

1. In 12-inch skillet, heat oil over medium heat and cook vegetables, stirring occasionally, 5 minutes or until tender.

2. Add chickpeas, raisins, soup mix blended with water, lemon juice and cumin. Cook, stirring occasionally, 3 minutes. Serve over hot couscous.

Makes about 4 servings

PREP TIME: 10 MINUTES
COOK TIME: 25 MINUTES

Ranch Mashed Potatoes

4 medium all-purpose potatoes, peeled, if desired, and cut into chunks (about 2 pounds)
1 envelope LIPTON® RECIPE SECRETS® Ranch Soup Mix
½ cup sour cream
½ cup milk
2 tablespoons margarine or butter, softened
2 slices bacon, crisp-cooked and crumbled *or* 2 tablespoons bacon bits (optional)

1. In 3-quart saucepan, cover potatoes with water. Bring to a boil.

2. Reduce heat to low and simmer 20 minutes or until potatoes are very tender; drain.

3. Return potatoes to saucepan; mash. Stir in remaining ingredients.

Makes 6 servings

Helpful Hint:
Store any remaining spread, covered, in the refrigerator for future use.

Onion-Herb Baked Bread

1 envelope LIPTON® RECIPE SECRETS® Golden Onion Soup Mix
1 medium clove garlic, finely chopped
1 teaspoon dried basil leaves
1 teaspoon dried oregano leaves
⅛ teaspoon black pepper
½ cup margarine or butter, softened
1 loaf Italian or French bread (about 16 inches long), halved lengthwise

1. Preheat oven to 375°F.

2. In small bowl, combine all ingredients except bread; generously spread on bread halves. Arrange bread, cut-side up, on baking sheet. Bake 15 minutes or until golden. Serve warm.

Makes 1 loaf

Golden Herb Stuffing

2 tablespoons I CAN'T BELIEVE IT'S NOT BUTTER!® Spread
1 medium carrot, diced
1 rib celery, diced
1 small onion, finely chopped
1 envelope LIPTON® RECIPE SECRETS® Savory Herb with Garlic
    Soup Mix
2 cups fresh bread crumbs
½ cup chopped walnuts or pecans (optional)
¼ cup milk or water

1. In 10-inch skillet, melt I Can't Believe It's Not Butter!® Spread over medium heat and cook carrot, celery and onion, stirring occasionally, 4 minutes.

2. In medium bowl, combine vegetables with remaining ingredients; toss well. Turn into 1-quart baking dish and bake covered, at 375°F for 25 minutes. Remove cover and bake an additional 5 minutes or until top is lightly browned. *Makes 4 servings*

Helpful Hint:
This recipe makes enough to stuff 1 roasting chicken, 2 Cornish hens, 8 pork chops or 8 fish fillets.

Creamy Ranch Dressing

1 envelope LIPTON® RECIPE SECRETS® Ranch Soup Mix
1 cup HELLMANN'S® or BEST FOODS® Real Mayonnaise or 1 cup
    sour cream
½ cup milk

1. In medium bowl, combine all ingredients. Chill 30 minutes.

2. Serve as dressing for salads and sandwiches.

Makes 1½ cups dressing

Helpful Hint:
Pour this dressing over tossed salad greens; use in your favorite pasta or potato salad; or use as a dressing for wraps and sandwiches.

PREP TIME: 10 MINUTES
COOK TIME: 10 MINUTES

Easy Fried Rice

¼ cup BERTOLLI® Olive Oil

4 cups cooked rice

2 cloves garlic, finely chopped

1 envelope LIPTON® RECIPE SECRETS® Onion Mushroom Soup Mix

½ cup water

1 tablespoon soy sauce

1 cup frozen peas and carrots, partially thawed

2 eggs, lightly beaten

1. In 12-inch nonstick skillet, heat oil over medium-high heat and cook rice, stirring constantly, 2 minutes or until rice is heated through. Stir in garlic.

2. Stir in soup mix blended with water and soy sauce and cook 1 minute. Stir in peas and carrots and cook 2 minutes or until heated through.

3. Make a well in center of rice and quickly stir in eggs until cooked.

Makes 4 servings

Simple Stuffed Potatoes

PREP TIME: 20 MINUTES
COOK TIME: 10 MINUTES

4 large baking potatoes, (about 12 ounces each), baked
1 envelope LIPTON® RECIPE SECRETS® Onion Soup Mix*
1 cup milk
4 tablespoons margarine or butter
½ cup shredded Cheddar cheese (about 2 ounces)

Also terrific with LIPTON® RECIPE SECRETS® Beefy Onion Soup Mix.

1. Preheat oven to 350°F. Cut potatoes in half lengthwise. Scoop pulp from each half and place in medium bowl. Add soup mix, milk and margarine; mash.

2. Spoon potato mixture back into potato shells. Sprinkle with cheese.

3. On baking sheet, arrange potatoes. Bake 10 minutes or until heated through and cheese is melted.   *Makes 4 servings*

Lipton® Onion Gravy

PREP TIME: 2 MINUTES
COOK TIME: 8 MINUTES

1 envelope LIPTON® RECIPE SECRETS® Onion Soup Mix*
2 tablespoons all-purpose flour
2 cups cold water

Also terrific with LIPTON® RECIPE SECRETS® Onion Mushroom or Beefy Onion Soup Mix.

1. In medium saucepan, combine soup mix and flour. Stir in water.

2. Bring to a boil over high heat, stirring occasionally.

3. Reduce heat to medium and simmer uncovered, stirring occasionally, 5 minutes or until gravy is thickened.   *Makes 2 cups gravy*

PREP TIME: 10 MINUTES
COOK TIME: 25 MINUTES

Easy "Baked" Beans

2 slices bacon, chopped

2 cans (19 ounces each) red kidney beans and/or cannellini beans, rinsed and drained

1 envelope LIPTON® RECIPE SECRETS® Beefy Onion Soup Mix

1½ cups water

¼ cup ketchup

2 tablespoons firmly packed brown sugar

1. In 3-quart saucepan, cook bacon over medium-high heat until crisp-tender. Stir in beans and cook, stirring frequently, 1 minute.

2. Stir in remaining ingredients. Bring to a boil over high heat.

3. Reduce heat to medium-low and simmer uncovered, 20 minutes or until thickened.   *Makes 6 servings*

PREP TIME: 5 MINUTES
COOK TIME: 25 MINUTES

Garlic Fries

1 bag (32 ounces) frozen French fried potatoes

1 envelope LIPTON® RECIPE SECRETS® Savory Herb with Garlic Soup Mix*

Also terrific with LIPTON® RECIPE SECRETS® Onion Soup Mix.

1. Preheat oven to 450°F. In large bowl, thoroughly toss frozen French fried potatoes with soup mix; spread on jelly-roll pan.

2. Bake until golden and crisp, about 25 minutes, stirring once.

Makes 4 servings

Simply Delicious Pasta Primavera

PREP TIME: 5 MINUTES
COOK TIME: 12 MINUTES

¼ cup margarine or butter

1 envelope LIPTON® RECIPE SECRETS® Vegetable Soup Mix

1½ cups milk

8 ounces linguine or spaghetti, cooked and drained

¼ cup grated Parmesan cheese (about 1 ounce)

1. In medium saucepan, melt margarine over medium heat; stir in soup mix and milk. Bring just to a boil over high heat.

2. Reduce heat to low and simmer uncovered, stirring occasionally, 10 minutes or until vegetables are tender. Toss hot linguine with sauce and Parmesan cheese.
Makes 4 servings

PREP TIME: 10 MINUTES
COOK TIME: 40 MINUTES

Onion-Roasted Potatoes

1 envelope LIPTON® RECIPE SECRETS® Onion Soup Mix*
4 medium all-purpose potatoes, cut into large chunks (about
    2 pounds)
⅓ cup BERTOLLI® Olive Oil

Also terrific with LIPTON® RECIPE SECRETS® Onion Mushroom, Golden Onion or Savory Herb with Garlic Soup Mix.

1. Preheat oven to 450°F. In 13×9-inch baking or roasting pan, combine all ingredients.

2. Bake uncovered, stirring occasionally, 40 minutes or until potatoes are tender and golden brown.   *Makes 4 servings*

Savory Lo Mein

2 tablespoons BERTOLLI® Olive Oil

1 medium clove garlic, finely chopped*

1 small head bok choy, cut into 2-inch pieces (about 5 cups)**

1 envelope LIPTON® RECIPE SECRETS® Onion Soup Mix***

1 cup water

2 tablespoons sherry (optional)

1 teaspoon soy sauce

¼ teaspoon ground ginger (optional)

8 ounces linguine or spaghetti, cooked and drained

*If using LIPTON® RECIPE SECRETS® Savory Herb with Garlic Soup Mix, omit garlic.

**Or use 5 cups coarsely shredded green cabbage. Decrease 10-minute cook time to 3 minutes.

***Also terrific with LIPTON® RECIPE SECRETS® Onion Mushroom, Savory Herb with Garlic or Golden Onion Soup Mix.

1. In 12-inch skillet, heat oil over medium heat and cook garlic and bok choy, stirring frequently, 10 minutes or until crisp-tender.

2. Stir in soup mix blended with water, sherry, soy sauce and ginger. Bring to a boil over high heat. Reduce heat to low and simmer uncovered, stirring occasionally, 5 minutes. Toss with hot linguine. Sprinkle, if desired, with toasted sesame seeds.   *Makes about 4 servings*

Vegetable Potato Salad

1 envelope LIPTON® RECIPE SECRETS® Vegetable Soup Mix
1 cup HELLMANN'S® or BEST FOODS® Real Mayonnaise
2 teaspoons white vinegar
2 pounds red or all-purpose potatoes, cooked and cut into chunks
¼ cup finely chopped red onion (optional)

1. In large bowl, combine soup mix, mayonnaise and vinegar.

2. Add potatoes and onion; toss well. Chill 2 hours.   *Makes 6 servings*

Roasted Vegetables with Fettuccine

2 pounds assorted fresh vegetables*

1 envelope LIPTON® RECIPE SECRETS® Savory Herb with Garlic
    Soup Mix**

3 tablespoons BERTOLLI® Olive Oil

½ cup light cream, whipping or heavy cream or half-and-half

¼ cup grated Parmesan cheese

8 ounces fettuccine or linguine, cooked and drained

*Use any combination of the following, cut into 1-inch chunks: zucchini; yellow
squash; red, green or yellow bell peppers; carrots; celery; onion or mushrooms.

**Also terrific with LIPTON® RECIPE SECRETS® Golden Onion Soup Mix.

1. Preheat oven to 450°F. In 13×9-inch baking or roasting pan, combine
vegetables, soup mix and oil until evenly coated.

2. Bake uncovered, stirring once, 20 minutes or until vegetables are
tender. Stir in cream and cheese until evenly coated.

3. Toss with hot fettuccine. Serve, if desired, with additional grated
Parmesan cheese and freshly ground black pepper.

Makes about 4 servings

Roasted Idaho & Sweet Potatoes

1 envelope LIPTON® RECIPE SECRETS® Onion Soup Mix
2 medium all-purpose potatoes, peeled, if desired, and cut into
    large chunks (about 1 pound)
2 medium sweet potatoes or yams, peeled, if desired, and cut into
    large chunks (about 1 pound)
¼ cup BERTOLLI® Olive Oil

1. Preheat oven to 425°F. In large plastic bag or bowl, combine all ingredients. Close bag and shake, or toss in bowl, until potatoes are evenly coated.

2. In 13×9-inch baking or roasting pan, arrange potatoes; discard bag.

3. Bake uncovered, stirring occasionally, 40 minutes or until potatoes are tender and golden.   *Makes 4 servings*

Confetti Rice Pilaf

1 tablespoon margarine or butter
1 cup regular or converted rice
1 cup fresh or drained canned sliced mushrooms
2 medium carrots, diced
1 envelope LIPTON® RECIPE SECRETS® Savory Herb with Garlic
    Soup Mix*
2¼ cups water

Also terrific with LIPTON® RECIPE SECRETS® Golden Onion, Onion Mushroom or Onion Soup Mix.

1. In 12-inch skillet, melt margarine over medium-high heat and cook rice, stirring frequently, until golden. Stir in mushrooms, carrots and soup mix blended with water. Bring to a boil over high heat.

2. Reduce heat to low and simmer covered, 20 minutes or until rice is tender.   *Makes 6 servings*

Roasted Idaho & Sweet Potatoes

FANTASTIC
BEEF & PORK

Home-cooked meals don't have to be complicated. With just a few ingredients and Lipton® Recipe Secrets® Soup Mix, you can serve great-tasting beef or pork entrées any night of the week. And with family-pleasers such as Easy Onion Tacos and Garlic Pork Chops, you won't have to worry about leftovers either!

Pizza Meat Loaf

1 envelope LIPTON® RECIPE SECRETS® Onion Soup Mix*
2 pounds ground beef
1½ cups fresh bread crumbs
2 eggs
1 small green bell pepper, chopped (optional)
¼ cup water
1 cup RAGÚ® Old World Style® Pasta Sauce, divided
1 cup shredded mozzarella cheese (about 4 ounces), divided

*Also terrific with LIPTON® RECIPE SECRETS® Savory Herb with Garlic Soup Mix.

1. Preheat oven to 350°F. In large bowl, combine all ingredients except ½ cup Pasta Sauce and ½ cup cheese.

2. In 13×9-inch baking or roasting pan, shape into loaf. Top with remaining ½ cup Pasta Sauce.

3. Bake uncovered, 50 minutes.

4. Sprinkle top with remaining ½ cup cheese. Bake an additional 10 minutes or until done. Let stand 10 minutes before serving.

Makes 8 servings

Helpful Hint:
When grating cheese, spray the box grater with nonstick cooking spray and place it on a sheet of waxed paper. Once done, simply discard the waxed paper and rinse the grater clean.

Pizza Meat Loaf

Helpful Hint:
To make this dish even easier to prepare, pick up pre-sliced vegetables from your local salad bar.

Chinese Pork & Vegetable Stir-Fry

2 tablespoons BERTOLLI® Olive Oil, divided

1 pound pork tenderloin or boneless beef sirloin, cut into 1/4-inch slices

6 cups assorted fresh vegetables*

1 can (8 ounces) sliced water chestnuts, drained

1 envelope LIPTON® RECIPE SECRETS® Onion Soup Mix

3/4 cup water

1/2 cup orange juice

1 tablespoon soy sauce

1/4 teaspoon garlic powder

Use any combination of the following: broccoli florets; thinly sliced red or green bell peppers; snow peas or thinly sliced carrots.

1. In 12-inch skillet, heat 1 tablespoon oil over medium-high heat; brown pork. Remove and set aside.

2. In same skillet, heat remaining 1 tablespoon oil and cook assorted fresh vegetables, stirring occasionally, 5 minutes. Stir in water chestnuts, soup mix blended with water, orange juice, soy sauce and garlic powder. Bring to a boil over high heat. Reduce heat to low and simmer uncovered, 3 minutes. Return pork to skillet and cook 1 minute or until heated through.

Makes about 4 servings

Harvest Pot Roast with Sweet Potatoes

1 envelope LIPTON® RECIPE SECRETS® Onion Soup Mix
1½ cups plus 3 tablespoons water, divided
¼ cup soy sauce
2 tablespoons firmly packed dark brown sugar
1 teaspoon ground ginger (optional)
1 (3- to 3½-pound) boneless pot roast (rump, chuck or round)
4 large sweet potatoes, peeled, if desired, and cut into large chunks
2 tablespoons all-purpose flour

1. Preheat oven to 325°F. In Dutch oven or 5-quart heavy ovenproof saucepan, combine soup mix, 1½ cups water, soy sauce, brown sugar and ginger; add roast.

2. Cover and bake 1 hour 45 minutes.

3. Add potatoes and bake covered, an additional 45 minutes or until beef and potatoes are tender.

4. Remove roast and potatoes to serving platter and keep warm; reserve juices.

5. In small cup, with wire whisk, blend remaining 3 tablespoons water and flour. In same Dutch oven, add flour mixture to reserved juices. Bring to a boil over high heat. Boil, stirring occasionally, 2 minutes. Serve with roast and potatoes. *Makes 6 servings*

Oniony Braised Short Ribs

2 tablespoons BERTOLLI® Olive Oil

3 pounds beef chuck short ribs

1 envelope LIPTON® RECIPE SECRETS® Onion Soup Mix

3½ cups water, divided

¼ cup ketchup

2 tablespoons firmly packed brown sugar

2 tablespoons sherry (optional)

½ teaspoon ground ginger

1 tablespoon all-purpose flour

¼ teaspoon black pepper

1. In 6-quart Dutch oven or saucepan, heat oil over medium-high heat and brown short ribs in two batches. Return ribs to Dutch oven.

2. Stir in soup mix blended with 3¼ cups water, ketchup, brown sugar, sherry and ginger. Bring to a boil. Reduce heat to low and simmer covered, 2 hours or until ribs are tender.

3. Remove ribs to serving platter and keep warm. In Dutch oven, add flour blended with remaining ¼ cup water and pepper. Bring to a boil over high heat. Boil, stirring occasionally, 2 minutes or until thickened. Pour sauce over ribs. Serve, if desired, with crusty bread.   *Makes 4 servings*

Slow Cooker Method: In slow cooker, arrange short ribs. Combine 2½ cups water with soup mix, ketchup, brown sugar, sherry and ginger; pour over ribs. Cook covered, on LOW 8 to 10 hours or HIGH 4 to 6 hours. Remove ribs to serving platter. Blend ¼ cup water with flour and pepper and stir into juices in slow cooker. Cook covered, on HIGH 15 minutes or until thickened. Pour over ribs.

Burger Pizzas Deluxe

PREP TIME: 5 MINUTES
COOK TIME: 25 MINUTES

1 pound ground beef
1 envelope LIPTON® RECIPE SECRETS® Onion Soup Mix
1½ cups water
1 cup RAGÚ® Old World Style® Pasta Sauce
2 cups shredded mozzarella cheese (about 8 ounces), divided
1 tablespoon grated Parmesan cheese
2 (12-inch) prebaked pizza crusts

Also terrific with LIPTON® RECIPE SECRETS® Beefy Onion or Onion Mushroom Soup Mix.

1. Preheat oven to 450°F. In 12-inch nonstick skillet, brown ground beef over medium-high heat; drain. Stir in soup mix blended with water and Pasta Sauce. Bring to a boil over high heat. Reduce heat to medium and cook 10 minutes.

2. Stir in 1 cup mozzarella cheese and Parmesan cheese. Evenly top pizza crusts with beef mixture, then remaining 1 cup mozzarella cheese.

3. On baking sheet, arrange pizzas and bake 10 minutes or until cheese is melted. *Makes 4 servings*

Easy Onion Tacos

PREP TIME: 5 MINUTES
COOK TIME: 15 MINUTES

1½ pounds ground beef
1 envelope LIPTON® RECIPE SECRETS® Onion Soup Mix
1½ cups salsa
1 package (4.8 ounces) taco shells, warmed, if desired

1. In 12-inch skillet, brown ground beef over medium-high heat; drain.

2. Stir in soup mix and salsa. Bring to a boil over high heat.

3. Reduce heat to low and simmer uncovered, stirring occasionally, 10 minutes or until thickened. Serve in warm taco shells. Top, if desired, with your favorite taco toppings. *Makes 10 tacos*

Onion-Baked Pork Chops

1 envelope LIPTON® RECIPE SECRETS® Golden Onion Soup Mix*
⅓ cup plain dry bread crumbs
4 pork chops, 1 inch thick (about 3 pounds)
1 egg, well beaten

Also terrific with LIPTON® RECIPE SECRETS® Onion or Savory Herb with Garlic Soup Mix.

1. Preheat oven to 400°F. In small bowl, combine soup mix and bread crumbs. Dip pork chops in egg, then bread crumb mixture until evenly coated.

2. On baking sheet, arrange pork chops.

3. Bake uncovered, 20 minutes or until done, turning once.

Makes 4 servings

FANTASTIC BEEF & PORK

Country-Style Pot Roast

PREP TIME: 10 MINUTES
COOK TIME: 2 HOURS
40 MINUTES

1 (3- to 3½-pound) boneless beef pot roast (rump, chuck or round)
1 envelope LIPTON® RECIPE SECRETS® Onion Soup Mix*
2½ cups water, divided
4 medium all-purpose potatoes, cut into 1-inch pieces (about
   2 pounds)
4 carrots, sliced
2 to 4 tablespoons all-purpose flour

*Also terrific with LIPTON® RECIPE SECRETS® Onion Mushroom or Beefy Onion
Soup Mix.

1. In Dutch oven or 6-quart saucepan, brown roast over medium-high heat.
Add soup mix blended with 2 cups water. Bring to a boil over high heat.
Reduce heat to low and simmer covered, turning roast occasionally,
2 hours.

2. Add vegetables and cook an additional 30 minutes or until vegetables
and roast are tender; remove roast and vegetables.

3. For gravy, blend remaining ½ cup water with flour; add to Dutch oven.
Bring to a boil over high heat. Reduce heat to low and simmer uncovered,
stirring constantly, about 5 minutes or until thickened.   *Makes 8 servings*

Slow Cooker Method: In slow cooker, add vegetables, then roast.
Add soup mix blended with 2 cups water. Cook covered, on LOW 8 to
10 hours or HIGH 4 to 6 hours or until roast is tender. Remove roast and
vegetables to serving platter. Blend remaining ½ cup water with flour and
stir into juices in slow cooker. Cook covered, on HIGH 15 minutes or until
thickened.

61

Asian Shrimp & Steak Kabobs

1 envelope LIPTON® RECIPE SECRETS® Savory Herb with Garlic or Onion Soup Mix

¼ cup soy sauce

¼ cup lemon juice

¼ cup BERTOLLI® Olive Oil

¼ cup honey

½ pound uncooked medium shrimp, peeled and deveined

½ pound boneless sirloin steak, cut into 1-inch cubes

16 cherry tomatoes

2 cups mushroom caps

1 medium green bell pepper, cut into chunks

1. In 13×9-inch glass baking dish, blend soup mix, soy sauce, lemon juice, oil and honey; set aside.

2. On skewers, alternately thread shrimp, steak, tomatoes, mushrooms and green pepper. Add prepared skewers to baking dish; turn to coat. Cover and marinate in refrigerator, turning skewers occasionally, at least 2 hours. Remove prepared skewers, reserving marinade.

3. Grill or broil, turning and basting frequently with reserved marinade, until shrimp turn pink and steak is cooked to desired doneness. Do not brush with marinade during last 5 minutes of cooking.   *Makes 4 servings*

Serving Suggestion: Serve with corn-on-the-cob, a mixed green salad and grilled garlic bread.

Souperior Meat Loaf

2 pounds ground beef

¾ cup plain dry bread crumbs*

1 envelope LIPTON® RECIPE SECRETS® Onion Soup Mix**

¾ cup water

⅓ cup ketchup

2 eggs

Substitution: Use 1½ cups fresh bread crumbs or 5 slices fresh bread, cubed.

**Also terrific with LIPTON® RECIPE SECRETS® Beefy Onion, Onion Mushroom or Savory Herb with Garlic Soup Mix.*

1. Preheat oven to 350°F. In large bowl, combine all ingredients.

2. In 13×9-inch baking or roasting pan, shape into loaf.

3. Bake uncovered, 1 hour or until done. Let stand 10 minutes before serving. *Makes 8 servings*

Slow Cooker Method: In slow cooker, arrange meat. Cook covered, on LOW 6 to 8 hours or HIGH for 4 hours. (Placing the meat loaf on a piece of cheesecloth and then on a rack helps to hold the loaf together while lifting it in and out of the slow cooker.)

Tip: It's a snap to make fresh bread crumbs. Simply process fresh or day old white, Italian or French bread in a food processor or blender until fine crumbs form.

Skillet Beef & Broccoli

PREP TIME: 10 MINUTES
COOK TIME: 15 MINUTES

    1 tablespoon BERTOLLI® Olive Oil
    1 pound sirloin steak, cut into 1-inch strips
    1 package (10 ounces) frozen broccoli florets, thawed
    1 envelope LIPTON® RECIPE SECRETS® Onion Soup Mix*
 1 ¼ cups water
    1 tablespoon firmly packed brown sugar
    1 tablespoon soy sauce
Also terrific with LIPTON® RECIPE SECRETS® Onion Mushroom Soup Mix.

1. In 12-inch nonstick skillet, heat oil over medium-high heat and brown steak, stirring occasionally, in two batches. Remove steak from skillet and set aside.

2. Stir in broccoli and soup mix blended with water, brown sugar and soy sauce. Bring to a boil over high heat. Reduce heat to low and simmer uncovered, stirring occasionally, 2 minutes.

3. Return steak to skillet and cook 1 minute or until steak is done. Serve, if desired, with hot cooked rice.   *Makes 4 servings*

FANTASTIC BEEF & PORK

PREP TIME: 5 MINUTES
COOK TIME: 25 MINUTES

Onion-Apple Glazed Pork Tenderloin

1 (1½- to 2-pound) boneless pork tenderloin
   Black pepper
2 tablespoons BERTOLLI® Olive Oil, divided
1 envelope LIPTON® RECIPE SECRETS® Onion Soup Mix
½ cup apple juice
2 tablespoons firmly packed brown sugar
¾ cup water
¼ cup dry red wine or water
1 tablespoon all-purpose flour

1. Preheat oven to 425°F. In small roasting pan or baking pan, arrange pork. Season with pepper and rub with 1 tablespoon oil. Roast uncovered, 10 minutes.

2. Meanwhile, in small bowl, combine remaining 1 tablespoon oil, soup mix, apple juice and brown sugar. Pour over pork and roast 10 minutes or until desired doneness. Remove pork to serving platter; cover with aluminum foil.

3. Place roasting pan over medium-high heat and bring pan juices to a boil, scraping up any browned bits from bottom of pan. Stir in water, wine and flour; boil, stirring constantly, 1 minute or until thickened.

4. To serve, thinly slice pork and serve with gravy.   *Makes 4 to 6 servings*

Helpful Hint:
Serve this hearty main dish with steak fries or baked potatoes.

Steaks with Peppers

2 tablespoons BERTOLLI® Olive Oil
1½ pounds boneless beef chuck steaks, ½ inch thick (about 4 to 5)
2 medium red, green and/or yellow bell peppers, cut into thin strips
1 clove garlic, finely chopped (optional)
1 medium tomato, coarsely chopped
1 envelope LIPTON® RECIPE SECRETS® Onion or Onion Mushroom Soup Mix
1 cup water

1. In 12-inch skillet, heat oil over medium-high heat and brown steaks. Remove steaks. Add peppers and garlic to skillet; cook over medium heat 5 minutes or until peppers are crisp-tender.

2. Stir in tomato, then soup mix blended with water; bring to a boil over high heat. Reduce heat to low. Return steaks to skillet and simmer uncovered, stirring sauce occasionally, 25 minutes or until steaks and vegetables are tender.   *Makes about 4 servings*

Buffalo Meat Loaf

1 envelope LIPTON® RECIPE SECRETS® Onion Soup Mix
2 pounds ground beef
1½ cups fresh bread crumbs
½ cup chopped celery
2 eggs
⅓ cup water
⅓ cup WISH-BONE® Blue Cheese Dressing
¼ cup hot pepper sauce

1. Preheat oven to 350°F. In large bowl, combine all ingredients.

2. In 13×9-inch baking or roasting pan, shape into loaf.

3. Bake uncovered, 1 hour or until done. Let stand 10 minutes before serving.   *Makes 8 servings*

Home-Style Beef Brisket

1 envelope LIPTON® RECIPE SECRETS® Onion Soup Mix*
¾ cup water
½ cup ketchup
1 teaspoon garlic powder
½ teaspoon black pepper
1 (3-pound) boneless brisket of beef

Also terrific with LIPTON® RECIPE SECRETS® Onion Mushroom, Beefy Onion or Savory Herb with Garlic Soup Mix.

1. Preheat oven to 325°F. In 13×9-inch baking or roasting pan, add soup mix blended with water, ketchup, garlic powder and pepper.

2. Add brisket; turn to coat.

3. Loosely cover with aluminum foil and bake 3 hours or until brisket is tender. If desired, thicken gravy.   *Makes 8 servings*

Helpful Hint:

For a quick one-dish dinner, during the last hour of baking add ½ pound carrots, cut into 2-inch pieces and 1 pound potatoes, peeled, if desired, and cut into 2-inch chunks.

PREP TIME: 10 MINUTES
COOK TIME: 1 HOUR

Southwestern Pork Roast

1 tablespoon BERTOLLI® Olive Oil
1 (2½-pound) boneless pork roast
1 can (14½ ounces) diced tomatoes
2 cans (4 ounces each) chopped green chilies, undrained
1 envelope LIPTON® RECIPE SECRETS® Onion Soup Mix
1 tablespoon firmly packed dark brown sugar
2 teaspoons to 1 tablespoon chili powder
1 teaspoon ground cumin

1. In Dutch oven, heat oil over medium-high heat. Brown pork roast on all sides, about 8 minutes. Stir in remaining ingredients.

2. Bring to a boil over high heat. Reduce heat to low and simmer covered, 50 minutes or until pork is done. Let stand 10 minutes. Serve, if desired, with hot cooked noodles or rice.   *Makes 4 to 6 servings*

Slow Cooker Method: In slow cooker, arrange pork. Combine remaining ingredients; pour over pork. Cook covered, on LOW 8 to 10 hours or HIGH 4 to 6 hours.

PREP TIME: 5 MINUTES
COOK TIME: 18 MINUTES

Steak Au Jus

1 (2-pound) boneless sirloin steak
1 envelope LIPTON® RECIPE SECRETS® Onion Soup Mix*
2 tablespoons BERTOLLI® Olive Oil
½ cup hot water

*Also terrific with LIPTON® RECIPE SECRETS® Savory Herb with Garlic, Ranch, Onion Mushroom or Beefy Onion Soup Mix.

1. In broiler pan, without the rack, arrange steak. Brush both sides of steak with soup mix blended with oil.

2. Broil steak until desired doneness, turning once.

3. Remove steak to serving platter. Add hot water to pan and stir, scraping brown bits from bottom. Serve sauce over steak.   *Makes 6 servings*

Savory Meatballs & Sauce

PREP TIME: 10 MINUTES
COOK TIME: 40 MINUTES

2 pounds ground beef
1 envelope LIPTON® RECIPE SECRETS® Onion Soup Mix
½ cup plain dry bread crumbs
1 jar (45 ounces) RAGÚ® Old World Style® Pasta Sauce, divided
1 tablespoon BERTOLLI® Olive Oil
1 pound spaghetti, cooked and drained

1. In large bowl, combine ground beef, soup mix, bread crumbs and ½ cup Pasta Sauce. Shape into 16 (2-inch) balls.

2. In large saucepan, heat oil over medium-high heat and cook half of the meatballs 6 minutes, turning once. Remove and set aside. Repeat with remaining meatballs.

3. Return meatballs to saucepan; add remaining Pasta Sauce. Gently stir to cover meatballs. Bring to a boil. Reduce heat to low and simmer covered, 35 minutes or until meatballs are done. Serve over hot cooked spaghetti.

Makes 4 servings

Herb-Crusted Roast Beef

1 envelope LIPTON® RECIPE SECRETS® Onion Soup Mix
½ cup plain dry bread crumbs
¼ cup I CAN'T BELIEVE IT'S NOT BUTTER!® Spread, melted
1 tablespoon prepared Dijon mustard
1 (3- to 4-pound) top round, rump or eye round roast

1. Preheat oven to 350°F. In small bowl, combine soup mix, bread crumbs, I Can't Believe It's Not Butter!® Spread and mustard.

2. In 13×9-inch baking or roasting pan, arrange roast on rack. Press soup mixture onto roast.

3. Bake uncovered, 1½ hours or until done. Garnish, if desired, with chopped fresh parsley.

Makes 6 servings

PREP TIME: 5 MINUTES
COOK TIME: 25 MINUTES

Garlic Pork Chops

6 bone-in pork chops, ¾ inch thick
1 envelope LIPTON® RECIPE SECRETS® Savory Herb with Garlic
    Soup Mix
2 tablespoons vegetable oil
½ cup hot water

1. Preheat oven to 425°F. In broiler pan, without the rack, arrange pork chops. Brush both sides of pork chops with soup mix blended with oil.

2. Bake pork chops 25 minutes or until done.

3. Remove pork chops to serving platter. Add hot water to pan and stir, scraping brown bits from bottom of pan. Serve sauce over pork chops.

Makes 4 servings

Tamale Pie

1 tablespoon BERTOLLI® Olive Oil

1 small onion, chopped

1 pound ground beef

1 envelope LIPTON® RECIPE SECRETS® Onion Soup Mix*

1 can (14½ ounces) stewed tomatoes, undrained

½ cup water

1 can (15 to 19 ounces) red kidney beans, rinsed and drained

1 package (8½ ounces) corn muffin mix, plus ingredients to prepare mix

Also terrific with LIPTON® RECIPE SECRETS® Onion Mushroom or Beefy Onion Soup Mix.

1. Preheat oven to 400°F.

2. In 12-inch skillet, heat oil over medium heat and cook onion, stirring occasionally, 3 minutes or until tender. Stir in ground beef and cook until browned.

3. Stir in soup mix blended with tomatoes and water. Bring to a boil over high heat, stirring with spoon to crush tomatoes. Reduce heat to low and stir in beans. Simmer uncovered, stirring occasionally, 10 minutes. Turn into 2-quart casserole.

4. Prepare corn muffin mix according to package directions. Spoon evenly over casserole.

5. Bake uncovered, 15 minutes or until corn topping is golden and filling is hot.

Makes 6 servings

Golden Glazed Flank Steak

    1 envelope LIPTON® RECIPE SECRETS® Onion Soup Mix*
    1 jar (12 ounces) apricot or peach preserves
    ½ cup water
    1 beef flank steak (about 2 pounds), cut into thin strips
    2 medium green, red and/or yellow bell peppers, sliced
       Hot cooked rice

Also terrific with LIPTON® RECIPE SECRETS® Onion Mushroom Soup Mix.

1. In small bowl, combine soup mix, preserves and water; set aside.

2. On foil-lined grid or in broiler pan, without the rack, arrange steak and bell peppers; top with soup mixture.

3. Grill or broil, turning steak and vegetables once, until steak is done. Serve over hot rice.   *Makes 8 servings*

Barbecued Meat Loaf

    1 envelope LIPTON® RECIPE SECRETS® Onion Soup Mix
    2 pounds ground beef
 1½ cups fresh bread crumbs
    2 eggs
    ¾ cup water
    ⅔ cup barbecue sauce, divided

1. Preheat oven to 350°F. In large bowl, combine all ingredients except ⅓ cup barbecue sauce.

2. In 13×9-inch baking or roasting pan, shape beef mixture into loaf. Top with reserved ⅓ cup barbecue sauce.

3. Bake uncovered, 1 hour or until done. Let stand 10 minutes before serving.   *Makes 8 servings*

INCREDIBLY
DELICIOUS
CHICKEN

Nothing brings your family together faster than dinner on the table. With irresistible favorites such as Easy Chicken Pot Pie, Spanish-Style Chicken & Rice, and Chicken Breasts with Savory Mustard Herb Sauce, they won't be in a hurry to leave.

Garlic Chicken Melt

- 4 boneless, skinless chicken breast halves (about 1¼ pounds)
- 1 envelope LIPTON® RECIPE SECRETS® Savory Herb with Garlic Soup Mix
- 1 can (14 ounces) diced tomatoes, undrained *or* 1 large tomato, chopped
- 1 tablespoon BERTOLLI® Olive Oil
- ½ cup shredded mozzarella or Monterey Jack cheese (about 2 ounces)

1. Preheat oven to 375°F. In 13×9-inch baking or roasting pan, arrange chicken. Pour soup mix blended with tomatoes and oil over chicken.

2. Bake uncovered, 25 minutes or until chicken is thoroughly cooked.

3. Sprinkle with mozzarella cheese and bake an additional 2 minutes or until cheese is melted.

Makes 4 servings

Garlic Chicken Melt

Helpful Hint:
Serve this savory and comforting pie with your favorite LIPTON® Iced Tea.

Easy Chicken Pot Pie

2 cups cut-up cooked chicken
1 package (10 ounces) frozen mixed vegetables, thawed
1¼ cups milk
1 envelope LIPTON® RECIPE SECRETS® Golden Onion Soup Mix*
1 pie crust or pastry for single-crust pie
Also terrific with LIPTON® RECIPE SECRETS® Savory Herb with Garlic Soup Mix.

1. Preheat oven to 400°F. In 9-inch pie plate, combine chicken and vegetables; set aside.

2. In small saucepan, bring milk and soup mix to a boil over medium heat, stirring occasionally. Cook 1 minute. Stir into chicken mixture.

3. Top with pie crust. Press pastry around edge of pie plate to seal; trim excess pastry, then flute edges. With tip of knife, make small slits in pastry.

4. Bake uncovered, 35 minutes or until crust is golden.

Makes about 4 servings

PREP TIME: 10 MINUTES
COOK TIME: 15 MINUTES

Golden Chicken Nuggets

1 envelope LIPTON® RECIPE SECRETS® Golden Onion Soup Mix
½ cup plain dry bread crumbs
1½ pounds boneless, skinless chicken breasts, cut into 2-inch pieces
2 tablespoons butter, melted
Also terrific with LIPTON® RECIPE SECRETS® Onion, Onion Mushroom or Savory Herb with Garlic Soup Mix.

1. Preheat oven to 425°F. In small bowl, combine soup mix and bread crumbs. Dip chicken in bread crumb mixture until evenly coated.

2. On lightly greased cookie sheet, arrange chicken; drizzle with butter.

3. Bake uncovered, 15 minutes or until chicken is thoroughly cooked, turning once.

Makes 6 servings

Herbed Chicken & Vegetables

2 medium all-purpose potatoes, thinly sliced (about 1 pound)

2 medium carrots, sliced

4 bone-in chicken pieces (about 2 pounds)

1 envelope LIPTON® RECIPE SECRETS® Savory Herb with Garlic Soup Mix

⅓ cup water

1 tablespoon BERTOLLI® Olive Oil

1. Preheat oven to 425°F. In broiler pan, without the rack, place potatoes and carrots; arrange chicken on top. Pour soup mix blended with water and oil over chicken and vegetables.

2. Bake uncovered, 40 minutes or until chicken is thoroughly cooked, juices run clear and vegetables are tender. *Makes 4 servings*

Slow Cooker Method: In slow cooker, layer potatoes, carrots then chicken. Pour soup mix blended with water and oil over chicken and vegetables. Cook covered, on LOW 6 to 8 hours or HIGH 4 hours.

Sesame Chicken

PREP TIME: 10 MINUTES
COOK TIME: 20 MINUTES

- 1 tablespoon BERTOLLI® Olive Oil
- 2 pounds boneless, skinless chicken breast halves (about 8)
- 1 envelope LIPTON® RECIPE SECRETS® Onion Soup Mix
- ¾ cup water
- 2 tablespoons orange juice
- 1 tablespoon firmly packed brown sugar
- 1 teaspoon sesame oil (optional)
- ½ teaspoon garlic powder
- 4 cups broccoli florets
- 1 teaspoon sesame seeds, toasted

1. In 12-inch nonstick skillet, heat oil over medium-high heat; add chicken and brown, turning once, 10 minutes. Stir in soup mix blended with water, juice, sugar, sesame oil and garlic powder. Bring to a boil; stir in broccoli.

2. Reduce heat to low and simmer covered, 8 minutes or until chicken is thoroughly cooked and broccoli is tender.

3. To serve, arrange on serving platter and sprinkle with sesame seeds.

Makes 4 servings

Sweet 'n' Spicy Chicken

- 1 bottle (8 ounces) WISH-BONE® Russian Dressing
- 1 envelope LIPTON® RECIPE SECRETS® Onion Soup Mix
- 1 jar (12 ounces) apricot preserves
- 1 (2½- to 3-pound) chicken, cut into serving pieces

1. Preheat oven to 425°F. In small bowl, combine Wish-Bone Russian Dressing, soup mix and preserves.

2. In 13×9-inch baking dish, arrange chicken; pour dressing mixture over chicken. Bake uncovered, basting occasionally, 40 minutes or until chicken is thoroughly cooked. Serve, if desired, with hot cooked rice.

Makes 6 servings

Crab-Stuffed Chicken Breasts

1 package (8 ounces) cream cheese, softened

6 ounces frozen crabmeat or imitation crabmeat, thawed and drained

1 envelope LIPTON® RECIPE SECRETS® Savory Herb with Garlic Soup Mix

6 boneless, skinless chicken breast halves (about 1 ½ pounds)

¼ cup all-purpose flour

2 eggs, beaten

¾ cup plain dry bread crumbs

2 tablespoons BERTOLLI® Olive Oil

1 tablespoon I CAN'T BELIEVE IT'S NOT BUTTER!® Spread

1. Preheat oven to 350°F. Combine cream cheese, crabmeat and soup mix; set aside. With knife parallel to cutting board, slice horizontally through each chicken breast, stopping 1 inch from opposite edge; open breasts. Evenly spread each breast with cream cheese mixture. Close each chicken breast, securing open edge with wooden toothpicks.

2. Dip chicken in flour, then eggs, then bread crumbs, coating well. In 12-inch skillet over medium-high heat, heat oil and I Can't Believe It's Not Butter!® Spread; cook chicken 10 minutes or until golden, turning once. Transfer chicken to 13×9-inch baking dish and bake uncovered, 15 minutes or until chicken is thoroughly cooked. Remove toothpicks before serving. *Makes about 6 servings*

Serving Suggestion: Serve with a mixed green salad and warm garlic bread.

Crab-Stuffed Chicken Breast

Helpful Hint:
*Recipes prepared in the
style of Provence, a region
in southeastern France,
are typically prepared with
garlic, tomatoes and olive
oil. Other ingredients
common to this region
include onions, olives,
mushrooms, anchovies and
eggplant.*

Roasted Chicken & Garlic Provençale

1 envelope LIPTON® RECIPE SECRETS® Savory Herb with Garlic
   Soup Mix
3 tablespoons BERTOLLI® Olive Oil
2 tablespoons water
1 tablespoon white wine vinegar (optional)
1 (2½- to 3-pound) chicken, cut into serving pieces
1 large onion, cut into 8 wedges
1 large tomato, cut into 8 wedges

1. Preheat oven to 425°F. In small bowl, combine soup mix, oil, water and
vinegar.

2. In broiler pan, without the rack, arrange chicken, onion and tomato.
Pour soup mixture over chicken and vegetables.

3. Roast 45 minutes or until chicken is thoroughly cooked.

Makes 4 servings

PREP TIME: 5 MINUTES
COOK TIME: 6 MINUTES

Ranch Chicken Tenders

2 tablespoons margarine or butter, melted
1 envelope LIPTON® RECIPE SECRETS® Ranch Soup Mix
1½ pounds chicken tenders or boneless, skinless chicken breast
   halves, cut into strips

1. In small bowl, combine margarine with soup mix. Add chicken to soup
mixture and let stand 5 minutes.

2. Heat 10-inch nonstick skillet over medium-high heat 3 minutes or until hot.

3. Add chicken mixture and cook, stirring occasionally, 6 minutes or until
chicken is thoroughly cooked. Serve, if desired, with your favorite dipping
sauce, or on buns with lettuce, tomato, mayonnaise or mustard, or in warm
flour tortillas with salsa.

Makes 4 servings

Roasted Chicken & Garlic Provençale

Chicken Tuscany

1 (2½- to 3-pound) chicken, cut into serving pieces
1 medium red or green bell pepper, cut into strips
1 jar (4½ ounces) sliced mushrooms, drained
1 envelope LIPTON® RECIPE SECRETS® Onion Soup Mix
1 can (14½ ounces) whole peeled tomatoes, undrained and chopped
½ cup orange juice or water
2 tablespoons firmly packed brown sugar
1 tablespoon BERTOLLI® Olive Oil (optional)

1. Preheat oven to 425°F. In 13×9-inch baking pan, arrange chicken, bell pepper and mushrooms; set aside.

2. In medium bowl, combine remaining ingredients; pour over chicken. Bake uncovered, 50 minutes or until chicken is thoroughly cooked.

Makes 4 servings

Lemon-Twist Chicken

2 tablespoons BERTOLLI® Olive Oil
4 boneless, skinless chicken breast halves (about 1¼ pounds)
1 envelope LIPTON® RECIPE SECRETS® Savory Herb with Garlic Soup Mix*
1¼ cups water
2 tablespoons lemon juice
1 tablespoon honey
1 teaspoon soy sauce

Also terrific with LIPTON® RECIPE SECRETS® Golden Onion Soup Mix.

1. In 12-inch skillet, heat oil over medium-high heat and brown chicken. Stir in soup mix blended with water, lemon juice, honey and soy sauce. Bring to a boil over high heat.

2. Reduce heat to low and simmer uncovered, 10 minutes or until chicken is thoroughly cooked. Serve, if desired, over hot cooked noodles or rice.

Makes 4 servings

Tortilla Crunch Chicken

1 envelope LIPTON® RECIPE SECRETS® Onion Soup Mix

1 cup finely crushed plain tortilla chips or cornflakes (about 3 ounces)

1 (2½- to 3-pound) chicken, cut into serving pieces (skinned, if desired) *or* 6 boneless, skinless chicken breast halves (about 1½ pounds)

1 egg

2 tablespoons water

2 tablespoons margarine or butter, melted

1. Preheat oven to 400°F.

2. In medium bowl, combine soup mix and tortilla chips. Dip chicken in egg beaten with water, then tortilla mixture, coating well. In 13×9-inch baking or roasting pan sprayed with nonstick cooking spray, arrange chicken; drizzle with margarine.

3. For chicken pieces, bake uncovered, 40 minutes or until chicken is thoroughly cooked. For chicken breast halves, bake uncovered, 15 minutes or until chicken is thoroughly cooked. *Makes 6 servings*

Helpful Hint:
Serve this crunchy chicken with your favorite fresh or store-bought salsa.

Helpful Hint:

A room temperature lemon will yield more juice than a cold lemon. To get even more juice, before squeezing it, roll the lemon on the countertop while pressing down on it with the palm of your hand.

Country French Chicken Breasts

2 tablespoons I CAN'T BELIEVE IT'S NOT BUTTER!® Spread

1 pound boneless, skinless chicken breast halves

1 envelope LIPTON® RECIPE SECRETS® Savory Herb with Garlic or Golden Onion Soup Mix

1 cup water

1 tablespoon lemon juice

Hot cooked rice

4 lemon slices (optional)

1. In 12-inch skillet, melt I Can't Believe It's Not Butter!® Spread over medium-high heat and brown chicken. Stir in soup mix blended with water and lemon juice. Reduce heat to low and simmer covered, 10 minutes or until sauce is slightly thickened and chicken is thoroughly cooked.

2. To serve, arrange chicken over hot rice and spoon sauce over chicken. Garnish, if desired, with lemon slices.   *Makes about 4 servings*

Easy Weeknight Chicken Cacciatore

PREP TIME: 10 MINUTES
COOK TIME: 40 MINUTES

    1 tablespoon BERTOLLI® Olive Oil
2 ½ pounds chicken pieces
    1 package (8 ounces) fresh mushrooms, sliced
    1 can (28 ounces) crushed tomatoes
    1 envelope LIPTON® RECIPE SECRETS® Onion Soup Mix
 ¼ cup dry red wine
 ½ teaspoon dried basil leaves

1. In 6-quart saucepan, heat oil over medium-high heat and brown chicken pieces. Add mushrooms and cook 2 minutes, stirring occasionally.

2. Stir in crushed tomatoes, soup mix, wine and basil. Bring to a boil over high heat.

3. Reduce heat to low and simmer covered, 30 minutes or until chicken is thoroughly cooked. Serve, if desired, over hot cooked noodles or rice.

Makes 4 servings

Slow Cooker Method: In slow cooker, add mushrooms, then chicken. Combine soup mix, tomatoes, wine and basil; pour over chicken. Cook covered, on LOW 8 hours or HIGH 4 to 6 hours.

Ranch Chicken Caesar Salad

8 cups torn romaine lettuce
Crispy Baked Ranch Chicken (recipe follows)
1 tomato, chopped
1 cup shredded Cheddar cheese (about 4 ounces)
¼ cup sliced pitted ripe olives
Creamy Ranch Dressing (recipe follows)

1. Divide lettuce evenly among 4 plates. Slice Crispy Baked Ranch Chicken and arrange over lettuce.

2. Sprinkle evenly with tomato, cheese and olives. Drizzle with Creamy Ranch Dressing. *Makes 4 servings*

Crispy Baked Ranch Chicken: Preheat oven to 425°F. In pie plate, combine 1 envelope LIPTON® RECIPE SECRETS® Ranch Soup Mix with ¾ cup plain dry bread crumbs. Brush 4 boneless, skinless chicken breast halves with ¼ cup HELLMANN'S® or BEST FOODS® Real Mayonnaise or sour cream, then evenly coat with soup mixture. In shallow baking pan, arrange chicken. Bake uncovered, 20 minutes or until chicken is thoroughly cooked.

Creamy Ranch Dressing: In medium bowl, combine 1 envelope LIPTON® RECIPE SECRETS® Ranch Soup Mix, 1 cup HELLMANN'S® or BEST FOODS® Real Mayonnaise or sour cream and ½ cup milk. Makes 1½ cups dressing.

Ranch Chicken Caesar Salad

Cheesy Garlic Chicken

Helpful Hint:

Turn leftover Cheesy Garlic Chicken into a quick and delicious lunch or dinner. Simply heat and serve it on hot store-bought garlic bread.

4 boneless, skinless chicken breast halves (about 1¼ pounds)

1 medium tomato, coarsely chopped

1 envelope LIPTON® RECIPE SECRETS® Savory Herb with Garlic Soup Mix

⅓ cup water

1 tablespoon BERTOLLI® Olive Oil

1 cup shredded mozzarella cheese (about 4 ounces)

1 tablespoon grated Parmesan cheese

1. Preheat oven to 400°F. In 13×9-inch baking dish, arrange chicken; top with tomato.

2. Pour soup mix blended with water and oil over chicken.

3. Bake uncovered, 20 minutes. Top with cheeses and bake 5 minutes or until cheese is melted and chicken is thoroughly cooked. Serve, if desired, with crusty Italian bread. *Makes 4 servings*

Spanish-Style Chicken & Rice

Helpful Hint:
Serve this tasty dish with
cooked green beans and
fresh fruit for dessert.

2 tablespoons BERTOLLI® Olive Oil

1 clove garlic, finely chopped

1 cup uncooked regular rice

1 envelope LIPTON® RECIPE SECRETS® Onion Soup Mix

2½ cups hot water

1 cup frozen peas, partially thawed

½ cup chopped red or green bell pepper

8 green olives, sliced

1 (2½- to 3-pound) chicken, cut into serving pieces

1. Preheat oven to 400°F.

2. In 13×9-inch baking or roasting pan, combine oil with garlic; heat in oven 5 minutes. Stir in uncooked rice until coated with oil. Add soup mix blended with hot water; stir in peas, bell pepper and olives. Press chicken pieces into rice mixture. Bake 35 minutes or until chicken is thoroughly cooked and rice is tender. Cover and let stand 10 minutes before serving.

Makes about 4 servings

Country Herb Roasted Chicken

1 (2½- to 3-pound) chicken, cut into serving pieces (with or without skin) *or* 1½ pounds boneless, skinless chicken breast halves

1 envelope LIPTON® RECIPE SECRETS® Savory Herb with Garlic Soup Mix

2 tablespoons water

1 tablespoon BERTOLLI® Olive Oil

1. Preheat oven to 375°F.

2. In 13×9-inch baking or roasting pan, arrange chicken. In small bowl, combine remaining ingredients; brush onto chicken.

3. For chicken pieces, bake uncovered, 45 minutes or until chicken is thoroughly cooked. For chicken breast halves, bake uncovered, 20 minutes or until chicken is thoroughly cooked.

Makes about 4 servings

Chicken Breasts Florentine

2 pounds boneless, skinless chicken breasts
¼ cup all-purpose flour
2 eggs, well beaten
⅔ cup seasoned dry bread crumbs
¼ cup BERTOLLI® Olive Oil
1 medium clove garlic, finely chopped
½ cup dry white wine
1 envelope LIPTON® RECIPE SECRETS® Golden Onion Soup Mix
1½ cups water
2 tablespoons finely chopped fresh parsley
⅛ teaspoon black pepper
   Hot cooked rice pilaf or white rice
   Hot cooked spinach

1. Dip chicken in flour, then eggs, then bread crumbs.

2. In 12-inch skillet, heat oil over medium heat and cook chicken until almost done. Remove chicken. Reserve 1 tablespoon drippings. Add garlic and wine to reserved drippings and cook over medium heat 5 minutes. Stir in soup mix blended with water; bring to a boil. Return chicken to skillet and simmer covered, 10 minutes or until chicken is thoroughly cooked and sauce is slightly thickened. Stir in parsley and pepper.

3. To serve, arrange chicken over hot rice and spinach; garnish as desired.   *Makes about 6 servings*

Cashew Chicken

1 tablespoon BERTOLLI® Olive Oil

1 pound boneless, skinless chicken breasts, cut into thin strips

1 envelope LIPTON® RECIPE SECRETS® Onion Soup Mix

¾ cup water

¼ cup firmly packed brown sugar

2 tablespoons sherry or water

1 tablespoon soy sauce

⅛ teaspoon ground ginger

1 package (16 ounces) frozen whole green beans, partially thawed

4 cups shredded iceberg lettuce

¼ cup chopped cashews or peanuts

1. In 12-inch nonstick skillet, heat oil over medium-high heat and brown chicken, stirring occasionally, 6 minutes or until chicken is thoroughly cooked. Remove chicken and keep warm.

2. In same skillet, stir in soup mix blended with water, brown sugar, sherry, soy sauce and ginger. Bring to a boil and continue boiling 3 minutes.

3. Add green beans and boil over medium heat 3 minutes. Return chicken to skillet and toss well.

4. To serve, arrange lettuce on serving platter; top with chicken and beans. Sprinkle with cashews. *Makes 4 servings*

Savory Chicken & Biscuits

2 tablespoons BERTOLLI® Olive Oil

1 pound boneless, skinless chicken breasts or thighs, cut into 1-inch pieces (about 2 cups)

1 medium onion, chopped

1 cup thinly sliced carrots

1 cup thinly sliced celery

1 envelope LIPTON® RECIPE SECRETS® Savory Herb with Garlic Soup Mix*

1 cup milk

1 package (10 ounces) refrigerated flaky buttermilk biscuits

*Also terrific with LIPTON® RECIPE SECRETS® Golden Onion Soup Mix.

1. Preheat oven to 375°F.

2. In 12-inch skillet, heat oil over medium-high heat and cook chicken, stirring occasionally, 5 minutes or until almost done. Stir in onion, carrots and celery; cook, stirring occasionally, 3 minutes. Stir in soup mix blended with milk. Bring to a boil over medium-high heat, stirring occasionally; cook 1 minute.

3. Turn into lightly greased 2-quart casserole; arrange biscuits on top of chicken mixture, with edges touching. Bake 10 minutes or until biscuits are golden brown.   *Makes 4 servings*

Helpful Hint:

Insert the meat thermometer into the thickest part of the thigh between the breast and the thigh. Make sure the tip of the thermometer does not touch bone.

Country Roasted Chicken Dinner

1 envelope LIPTON® RECIPE SECRETS® Savory Herb with Garlic Soup Mix*

2 tablespoons honey

1 tablespoon water

1 tablespoon I CAN'T BELIEVE IT'S NOT BUTTER!® Spread, melted

1 (5- to 6-pound) roasting chicken

3 pounds all-purpose and/or sweet potatoes, cut into chunks

Also terrific with LIPTON® RECIPE SECRETS® Golden Onion Soup Mix.

1. Preheat oven to 350°F.

2. In small bowl, blend soup mix, honey, water and I Can't Believe It's Not Butter!® Spread.

3. In 18×12-inch roasting pan, arrange chicken, breast side up; brush with soup mixture. Cover loosely with aluminum foil. Roast 30 minutes; drain off drippings. Arrange potatoes around chicken and roast covered, stirring potatoes occasionally, 1 hour or until meat thermometer reaches 175°F and potatoes are tender. *If chicken reaches 175°F before potatoes are tender, remove chicken to serving platter and keep warm. Continue roasting potatoes until tender.*　　　　*Makes about 8 servings*

Serving Suggestion: Serve with a mixed green salad, warm biscuits and LIPTON® Iced Tea.

Grilled Garlic Chicken

1 envelope LIPTON® RECIPE SECRETS® Savory Herb with Garlic Soup Mix
3 tablespoons BERTOLLI® Olive Oil
4 boneless, skinless chicken breast halves (about 1¼ pounds)

1. In medium bowl, combine soup mix with oil.

2. Add chicken; toss to coat.

3. Grill or broil until chicken is thoroughly cooked.   *Makes 4 servings*

Chicken Breasts with Savory Mustard Herb Sauce

2 tablespoons BERTOLLI® Olive Oil, divided
1 pound boneless, skinless chicken breast halves
1 medium zucchini, sliced
1½ cups sliced fresh or drained canned mushrooms
1 envelope LIPTON® RECIPE SECRETS® Savory Herb with Garlic or Golden Onion Soup Mix
¾ cup water
2 teaspoons prepared Dijon, country Dijon or brown mustard

1. In 12-inch skillet, heat 1 tablespoon oil over medium-high heat; cook chicken 5 minutes or until almost done, turning once. Remove; keep warm.

2. In same skillet, heat remaining 1 tablespoon oil over medium heat and cook zucchini and mushrooms, stirring frequently, 3 minutes. Return chicken to skillet; stir in soup mix blended with water and mustard. Bring to a boil over high heat. Reduce heat to low and simmer covered, 5 minutes or until chicken is thoroughly cooked.

3. To serve, arrange chicken on serving platter and top with sauce mixture.
Makes 4 servings

HEARTY
SOUPS, STEWS
& SANDWICHES

When you've got a hungry family to feed, there is no need to turn to frozen dinners or take-out food. Even the largest appetite can be satisfied with a big bowl of piping hot Meatball & Pasta Soup, stick-to-your-ribs Oven-Baked Stew or Philly-Style Cheese Steak sandwiches.

Hearty BBQ Beef Sandwiches

1 envelope LIPTON® RECIPE SECRETS® Onion Soup Mix
2 cups water
½ cup chili sauce
¼ cup firmly packed light brown sugar
1 (3-pound) boneless chuck roast
8 kaiser rolls or hamburger buns, toasted

1. Preheat oven to 325°F. In Dutch oven or 5-quart heavy ovenproof saucepan, combine soup mix, water, chili sauce and sugar; add roast.

2. Cover and bake 3 hours or until roast is tender.

3. Remove roast; reserve juices. Bring reserved juices to a boil over high heat. Boil 4 minutes.

4. Meanwhile, with fork, shred roast. Stir roast into reserved juices and simmer, stirring frequently, 1 minute. Serve on rolls.   *Makes 8 servings*

Helpful Hint:

Always measure brown sugar in a dry measure cup and pack it down firmly. To soften hardened brown sugar, place it in a glass dish with 1 slice of bread. Cover with plastic wrap and microwave at HIGH 30 to 40 seconds. Let stand about 30 seconds; stir. Remove bread.

Hearty BBQ Beef Sandwich

Southwestern Beef Stew

1 tablespoon plus 1 teaspoon BERTOLLI® Olive Oil, divided
1½ pounds boneless beef chuck, cut into 1-inch cubes
1 can (4 ounces) chopped green chilies, drained
2 large cloves garlic, finely chopped
1 teaspoon ground cumin (optional)
1 can (14 to 16 ounces) whole or plum tomatoes, undrained and chopped
1 envelope LIPTON® RECIPE SECRETS® Onion or Beefy Onion Soup Mix
1 cup water
1 package (10 ounces) frozen cut okra or green beans, thawed
1 large red or green bell pepper, cut into 1-inch pieces
4 frozen half-ears corn-on-the-cob, thawed and each cut into 3 round pieces
2 tablespoons chopped fresh cilantro (optional)

1. In 5-quart Dutch oven or heavy saucepan, heat 1 tablespoon oil over medium-high heat and brown half of the beef; remove and set aside. Repeat with remaining beef; remove and set aside.

2. In same Dutch oven, heat remaining 1 teaspoon oil over medium heat and cook chilies, garlic and cumin, stirring constantly, 3 minutes. Return beef to Dutch oven. Stir in tomatoes and soup mix blended with water. Bring to a boil over high heat. Reduce heat to low and simmer covered, stirring occasionally, 1 hour.

3. Stir in okra, bell pepper and corn. Bring to a boil over high heat. Reduce heat to low and simmer covered, stirring occasionally, 30 minutes or until meat is tender. Sprinkle with cilantro. *Makes 6 servings*

Southwestern Beef Stew

Cheesy Spinach Burgers

1 envelope LIPTON® RECIPE SECRETS® Onion Soup Mix
2 pounds ground beef
1 package (10 ounces) frozen chopped spinach, thawed and
   squeezed dry
1 cup shredded mozzarella or Cheddar cheese (about 4 ounces)

1. In large bowl, combine all ingredients; shape into 8 patties.

2. Grill or broil until no longer pink in center (160°F). Serve, if desired, on
hamburger buns.   *Makes 8 servings*

Hearty Lentil Stew

2 tablespoons BERTOLLI® Olive Oil
3 medium carrots, sliced
3 ribs celery, sliced
1 cup lentils, rinsed and drained
3 cups water, divided
1 envelope LIPTON® RECIPE SECRETS® Savory Herb with Garlic
   Soup Mix*
1 tablespoon cider vinegar or red wine vinegar (optional)
   Hot cooked brown rice, couscous or pasta
Also terrific with LIPTON® RECIPE SECRETS® Onion Mushroom or Onion Soup Mix.

1. In 3-quart saucepan, heat oil over medium heat and cook carrots and
celery, stirring occasionally, 3 minutes.

2. Add lentils and cook 1 minute. Stir in 2 cups water. Bring to a boil over
high heat. Reduce heat to low and simmer covered, stirring occasionally,
25 minutes.

3. Stir in soup mix blended with remaining 1 cup water. Simmer covered,
additional 10 minutes or until lentils are tender. Stir in vinegar. Serve over
hot rice.   *Makes about 4 servings*

Cheesy Spinach Burgers

Lentil and Brown Rice Soup

1 envelope LIPTON® RECIPE SECRETS® Onion Soup Mix*
4 cups water
¾ cup lentils, rinsed and drained
½ cup uncooked brown or regular rice
1 can (14½ ounces) whole peeled tomatoes, undrained and
   coarsely chopped
1 medium carrot, coarsely chopped
1 large stalk celery, coarsely chopped
½ teaspoon dried basil leaves
½ teaspoon dried oregano leaves
¼ teaspoon dried thyme leaves (optional)
1 tablespoon finely chopped fresh parsley
1 tablespoon apple cider vinegar
¼ teaspoon black pepper

*Also terrific with LIPTON® RECIPE SECRETS® Beefy Onion Soup Mix.

1. In large saucepan or stockpot, combine soup mix, water, lentils, uncooked rice, tomatoes with liquid, carrot, celery, basil, oregano and thyme.

2. Bring to a boil, then simmer covered, stirring occasionally, 45 minutes or until lentils and rice are tender. Stir in remaining ingredients.

Makes 3 (2-cup) servings

Onion Sloppy Joes

1½ pounds ground beef
1 envelope LIPTON® RECIPE SECRETS® Onion Soup Mix
1 cup water
1 cup ketchup
2 tablespoons firmly packed light brown sugar

1. In 10-inch skillet, brown ground beef over medium-high heat; drain.

2. Stir in remaining ingredients. Bring to a boil over high heat.

3. Reduce heat to low and simmer uncovered, stirring occasionally, 8 minutes or until mixture thickens. Serve, if desired, on hoagie rolls or hamburger buns.   *Makes about 6 servings*

Serving Suggestion: Serve with a lettuce and tomato salad, tortilla chips and ice cream with a choice of toppings.

Tempting Taco Burgers

1 envelope LIPTON® RECIPE SECRETS® Onion Mushroom Soup Mix*
1 pound ground beef
½ cup chopped tomato
¼ cup finely chopped green bell pepper
1 teaspoon chili powder
¼ cup water

Also terrific with LIPTON® RECIPE SECRETS® Onion or Beefy Onion Soup Mix.

1. In large bowl, combine all ingredients; shape into 4 patties.

2. Grill or broil until no longer pink in center (160°F). Serve, if desired, on hamburger buns and top with shredded lettuce and Cheddar cheese.

Makes 4 servings

Helpful Hint:

The best way to test for doneness of beef, pork and poultry is to use a meat thermometer or an instant read thermometer. But, you may want to try this quick touch test first: Gently press a piece of uncooked flesh to feel what rare feels like; the flesh will become tighter and more resistant as it cooks. Medium will have some give; well-done will be quite firm.

Oven-Baked Stew

2 pounds boneless beef chuck or round steak, cut into 1-inch cubes
¼ cup all-purpose flour
1⅓ cups sliced carrots
1 can (14 to 16 ounces) whole peeled tomatoes, undrained and chopped
1 envelope LIPTON® RECIPE SECRETS® Onion Soup Mix*
½ cup dry red wine or water
1 cup fresh or canned sliced mushrooms
1 package (8 ounces) medium or broad egg noodles, cooked and drained

Also terrific with LIPTON® RECIPE SECRETS® Beefy Onion or Onion Mushroom Soup Mix.

1. Preheat oven to 425°F. In 2½-quart shallow casserole, gently toss beef with flour, then bake uncovered, 20 minutes, stirring once.

2. *Reduce heat to 350°F.* Stir in carrots, tomatoes, soup mix and wine.

3. Bake covered, 1½ hours or until beef is tender. Stir in mushrooms and bake covered, an additional 10 minutes. Serve over hot noodles.

Makes 8 servings

Slow Cooker Method: In slow cooker, gently toss beef with flour. Add carrots, tomatoes, soup mix and wine. Cook covered, on LOW 8 to 10 hours. Add mushrooms; cook covered, on LOW 30 minutes or until beef is tender. Serve over hot noodles.

Grilled Vegetable Sandwiches

2 pounds assorted fresh vegetables*
1 envelope LIPTON® RECIPE SECRETS® Onion Soup Mix**
⅓ cup BERTOLLI® Olive Oil
2 tablespoons balsamic or red wine vinegar
½ teaspoon dried basil leaves, crushed
4 (8-inch) pita breads, warmed
4 ounces crumbled Montrachet, shredded mozzarella, Jarlsberg, Monterey Jack or Cheddar cheese

*Use any combination of the following, sliced: red, green or yellow bell peppers; mushrooms; zucchini or eggplant.
**Also terrific with LIPTON® RECIPE SECRETS® Onion, Savory Herb with Garlic or Golden Onion Soup Mix.

1. In large bowl, combine vegetables and soup mix blended with oil, vinegar and basil until evenly coated.

2. Grill or broil vegetables until tender. To serve, cut 1-inch strip off each pita. Fill with vegetables and sprinkle with cheese. Garnish, if desired, with shredded lettuce and sliced tomato. *Makes 4 servings*

PREP TIME: 10 MINUTES
COOK TIME: 8 MINUTES

Chicken Fajitas

2 tablespoons BERTOLLI® Olive Oil
2 medium red and/or green bell peppers, sliced
1 pound boneless, skinless chicken breasts, sliced
1 envelope LIPTON® RECIPE SECRETS® Onion Soup Mix
½ cup water
Flour tortillas, warmed

1. In 12-inch nonstick skillet, heat oil over medium-high heat and cook bell peppers 2 minutes. Add chicken and cook 4 minutes or until lightly browned.

2. Stir in soup mix blended with water. Simmer 2 minutes or until chicken is thoroughly cooked. Serve in warm tortillas. *Makes 4 servings*

Garden Burgers

1½ pounds ground beef or turkey

1 envelope LIPTON® RECIPE SECRETS® Onion Soup Mix*

2 small carrots, finely shredded

1 small zucchini, shredded

1 egg, lightly beaten

¼ cup plain dry bread crumbs

Also terrific with LIPTON® RECIPE SECRETS® Savory Herb with Garlic or Onion Mushroom Soup Mix.

1. In large bowl, combine all ingredients; shape into 6 patties.

2. Grill or broil until no longer pink in center (160°F). Serve, if desired, on hamburger buns or whole wheat rolls.   *Makes 6 servings*

Seafood Salad Sandwiches

1 envelope LIPTON® RECIPE SECRETS® Vegetable Soup Mix
¾ cup sour cream
½ cup chopped celery
¼ cup HELLMANN'S® or BEST FOODS® Real Mayonnaise
1 tablespoon fresh or frozen chopped chives (optional)
1 teaspoon lemon juice
   Hot pepper sauce to taste
⅛ teaspoon black pepper
2 packages (6 ounces each) frozen crabmeat, thawed and well
   drained
4 hard rolls, halved
   Lettuce leaves

1. In large bowl, combine soup mix, sour cream, celery, mayonnaise, chives, lemon juice, hot pepper sauce and black pepper. Stir in crabmeat; chill.

2. To serve, line rolls with lettuce, then fill with crab mixture.

Makes 4 sandwiches

Variations: Use 1 package (12 ounces) frozen cleaned shrimp, cooked and coarsely chopped; or 2 packages (8 ounces each) sea legs, thawed, drained and chopped; or 1 can (12 ounces) tuna, drained and flaked; or 2 cans (about 4 ounces each) medium or large shrimp, drained and chopped; or 2 cans (6 ounces each) crabmeat, drained and flaked.

Seafood Salad Sandwiches

Country Italian Soup

1 tablespoon BERTOLLI® Olive Oil

½ pound boneless beef, cut into 1-inch cubes

1 can (14½ ounces) whole peeled tomatoes, undrained and chopped

1 envelope LIPTON® RECIPE SECRETS® Onion Soup Mix

3 cups water

1 medium onion, cut into chunks

1 large rib celery, cut into 1-inch pieces

½ cup sliced carrot

1 cup cut green beans

1 can (16 ounces) chick-peas or garbanzos, rinsed and drained

½ cup sliced zucchini

¼ cup uncooked elbow macaroni

¼ teaspoon dried oregano leaves

1. In large saucepan or stockpot, heat oil over medium-high heat and brown beef. Add tomatoes, then soup mix blended with water. Simmer uncovered, stirring occasionally, 30 minutes.

2. Add onion, celery, carrot and green beans. Simmer uncovered, stirring occasionally, 30 minutes.

3. Stir in remaining ingredients and simmer uncovered, stirring occasionally, an additional 15 minutes or until vegetables and macaroni are tender. Serve, if desired, with grated Parmesan cheese.

Makes about 8 (1-cup) servings

Philly-Style Cheese Steaks

PREP TIME: 5 MINUTES
COOK TIME: 5 MINUTES

1 pound minute or cubed steaks
1 envelope LIPTON® RECIPE SECRETS® Onion Soup Mix
½ cup water
4 hoagie or Italian rolls, split
1 cup shredded Cheddar cheese (about 4 ounces)

1. In 10-inch skillet, cook steaks over medium-high heat 2 minutes or until desired doneness, turning once. Remove steaks and keep warm.

2. In same skillet, add soup mix blended with water; cook 2 minutes. Return steaks to skillet and cook 1 minute or until heated through. To serve, arrange steaks on rolls; top with sauce and Cheddar cheese.

Makes 4 servings

Meatball & Pasta Soup

PREP TIME: 10 MINUTES
COOK TIME: 15 MINUTES

2 cans (14½ ounces each) chicken broth
4 cups water
1 can (15 ounces) crushed tomatoes
1 package (15 ounces) frozen precooked Italian style meatballs, not in sauce
1 envelope LIPTON® RECIPE SECRETS® Onion Soup Mix
½ teaspoon garlic powder
1 cup uncooked mini pasta (such as conchigliette or ditalini)
4 cups fresh baby spinach leaves

Helpful Hint:
For a real flavor boost, try using LIPTON® RECIPE SECRETS® Soup Mix as a dry rub; try it on chicken, steak, pork or vegetables. You can even rub it on hamburgers before cooking.

1. In 6-quart saucepan, bring broth, water, crushed tomatoes, meatballs, soup mix and garlic powder to a boil over medium-high heat.

2. Add pasta and cook 5 minutes or until pasta is almost tender. Stir in spinach. Reduce heat to medium and simmer uncovered, 2 minutes or until spinach is wilted and pasta is tender. Serve, if desired, with Parmesan cheese.

Makes 8 servings

Country Chicken Stew with Dumplings

1 tablespoon BERTOLLI® Olive Oil
1 (3- to 3½-pound) chicken, cut into serving pieces (with or without skin)
4 large carrots, cut into 2-inch pieces
3 ribs celery, cut into 1-inch pieces
1 large onion, cut into 1-inch wedges
1 envelope LIPTON® RECIPE SECRETS® Savory Herb with Garlic Soup Mix*
1½ cups water
½ cup apple juice
Parsley Dumplings (optional, recipe follows)
Also terrific with LIPTON® RECIPE SECRETS® Golden Onion Soup Mix.

1. In 6-quart Dutch oven or heavy saucepan, heat oil over medium-high heat and brown half of the chicken; remove and set aside. Repeat with remaining chicken. Return chicken to Dutch oven. Stir in carrots, celery, onion, soup mix blended with water and apple juice. Bring to a boil over high heat. Reduce heat to low; simmer covered, 25 minutes or until chicken is thoroughly cooked, juices run clear and vegetables are tender.

2. Meanwhile, prepare Parsley Dumplings. Drop 12 rounded tablespoonfuls of batter into simmering broth around chicken. Simmer covered, 10 minutes or until toothpick inserted into center of dumplings comes out clean. Season stew, if desired, with salt and black pepper.

Makes about 6 servings

Parsley Dumplings: In medium bowl, combine 1⅓ cups all-purpose flour, 2 teaspoons baking powder, 1 tablespoon chopped fresh parsley and ½ teaspoon salt; set aside. In measuring cup, blend ⅔ cup milk, 2 tablespoons melted butter or margarine and 1 egg. Stir milk mixture into flour mixture just until blended.

Variation: Add 1 pound quartered red potatoes to stew with carrots; omit dumplings.

PREP TIME: 10 MINUTES
COOK TIME: 12 MINUTES

Lipton® Onion Burgers

1 envelope LIPTON® RECIPE SECRETS® Onion Soup Mix*

2 pounds ground beef

½ cup water

Also terrific with LIPTON® RECIPE SECRETS® Beefy Onion, Onion Mushroom, Savory Herb with Garlic or Ranch Soup Mix.

1. In large bowl, combine all ingredients; shape into 8 patties.

2. Grill or broil until done. *Makes 8 servings*

Hearty White Bean Soup

1 tablespoon BERTOLLI® Olive Oil

1 medium onion, chopped

2 medium carrots, sliced

2 ribs celery, sliced

1 clove garlic

2 cans (about 19 ounces each) cannellini or white kidney beans, rinsed and drained

1 envelope LIPTON® RECIPE SECRETS® Savory Herb with Garlic Soup Mix

2 cups water

3 cups coarsely chopped escarole or spinach

1 medium tomato, diced

¼ cup crumbled feta cheese (optional)

1. In 3-quart saucepan, heat oil over medium heat and cook onion, carrots, celery and garlic, stirring occasionally, 5 minutes or until tender.

2. Stir in beans and soup mix blended with water. Bring to a boil over high heat. Reduce heat to low and simmer uncovered, 15 minutes or until vegetables are tender.

3. Stir in escarole and tomato and cook 2 minutes or until heated through. Top with cheese. *Makes about 6 cups soup*

Lipton® Onion Burgers

Index

Metric Conversion Chart

VOLUME MEASUREMENTS (dry)

¹/₈ teaspoon = 0.5 mL
¹/₄ teaspoon = 1 mL
¹/₂ teaspoon = 2 mL
³/₄ teaspoon = 4 mL
1 teaspoon = 5 mL
1 tablespoon = 15 mL
2 tablespoons = 30 mL
¹/₄ cup = 60 mL
¹/₃ cup = 75 mL
¹/₂ cup = 125 mL
²/₃ cup = 150 mL
³/₄ cup = 175 mL
1 cup = 250 mL
2 cups = 1 pint = 500 mL
3 cups = 750 mL
4 cups = 1 quart = 1 L

VOLUME MEASUREMENTS (fluid)

1 fluid ounce (2 tablespoons) = 30 mL
4 fluid ounces (¹/₂ cup) = 125 mL
8 fluid ounces (1 cup) = 250 mL
12 fluid ounces (1¹/₂ cups) = 375 mL
16 fluid ounces (2 cups) = 500 mL

WEIGHTS (mass)

¹/₂ ounce = 15 g
1 ounce = 30 g
3 ounces = 90 g
4 ounces = 120 g
8 ounces = 225 g
10 ounces = 285 g
12 ounces = 360 g
16 ounces = 1 pound = 450 g

DIMENSIONS

¹/₁₆ inch = 2 mm
¹/₈ inch = 3 mm
¹/₄ inch = 6 mm
¹/₂ inch = 1.5 cm
³/₄ inch = 2 cm
1 inch = 2.5 cm

OVEN TEMPERATURES

250°F = 120°C
275°F = 140°C
300°F = 150°C
325°F = 160°C
350°F = 180°C
375°F = 190°C
400°F = 200°C
425°F = 220°C
450°F = 230°C

BAKING PAN SIZES

Utensil	Size in Inches/Quarts	Metric Volume	Size in Centimeters
Baking or	8×8×2	2 L	20×20×5
Cake Pan	9×9×2	2.5 L	23×23×5
(square or	12×8×2	3 L	30×20×5
rectangular)	13×9×2	3.5 L	33×23×5
Loaf Pan	8×4×3	1.5 L	20×10×7
	9×5×3	2 L	23×13×7
Round Layer	8×1½	1.2 L	20×4
Cake Pan	9×1½	1.5 L	23×4
Pie Plate	8×1¼	750 mL	20×3
	9×1¼	1 L	23×3
Baking Dish	1 quart	1 L	—
or Casserole	1½ quart	1.5 L	—
	2 quart	2 L	—